MW01056186

Process Quality
Management & Improvement
Guidelines

Issue 1.1

AT&T Quality Steering Committee

For more information on consulting services and training
in the methods and tools described in this book,
contact the AT&T Quality Helpline at **1-908-204-1099**.

Additional copies of 500-049 may be ordered from:

AT&T's Customer Information Center
Order Entry Department
P.O. Box 19901
Indianapolis, IN 46219
1-800-432-6600
1-800-255-1242 Canada
1-317-322-6646 International
1-317-322-6416 International
1-317-322-6699 International Fax

ISBN 0-932764-32-0

Prepared by the Publication Center
AT&T Bell Laboratories

AT&T Quality Policy

Quality excellence is the foundation for the management of our business and the keystone of our goal of customer satisfaction. It is, therefore, our policy to:

- Consistently provide products and services that meet the quality expectations of our customers.

- Actively pursue ever-improving quality through programs that enable each employee to do his or her job right the first time.

Robert E. Allen
Chairman of the Board and Chief Executive Officer

PREFACE

Quality...lies at the heart of everything we do...we will dedicate ourselves to continually improving the quality of our products and services by focusing on our processes and procedures.

AT&T Quality Policy, Intent Section

The AT&T Quality Policy defines a responsibility for each AT&T employee to contribute to the realization of AT&T's goal of customer satisfaction. The AT&T Quality Steering Committee recognized the need for a set of guidelines to help managers implement the Quality Policy within their processes. To address this need, the committee sponsored the development of the *Process Quality Management and Improvement Guidelines.*

The methods and procedures outlined in these guidelines are based on quality management practices that have proven effective in AT&T and other companies. Applying these procedures will help managers increase the effectiveness and efficiency of their processes and, consequently, achieve a higher level of customer satisfaction and reduce costs. Although the guidelines were designed for process owners and managers, the concepts and techniques are useful to all employees.

The AT&T Quality Steering Committee

Phil Scanlan, Chairman	Ray Peterson
Donald Conover	Thomas Roose
Joe Crupi	Vince Salvati
Ed Fuchs	Stan Seibert
Bill Kastning	Dick Shahpazian
Lex McCusker	Bill Thompson
Joel Moses	Jay Walters
Bill Mullane	

Authors

Roger Ackerman
Roberta Coleman
Elias Leger
John MacDorman

ACKNOWLEDGMENTS

The AT&T Quality Steering Committee sponsored the development and writing of the *Process Quality Management and Improvement Guidelines* (Issue 1), authored by:

> Elias Leger, Project Leader
> Roger Ackerman
> Roberta Coleman
> John MacDorman

The authors are indebted to the many individuals who helped to create this book. Ian Durand introduced the concept of process quality management in AT&T, and Bob Kerwin provided the support for documenting the methodology. Greg Shaw provided technical supervision and, with Ramon Leon, was available for ongoing technical consultation. Bill Comella and Alex David acted as mentors in producing these guidelines.

The authors also extend their appreciation to Susan Annitto, April Cormaci, and Mari-Lynn Hankinson for their help in writing, editing, and producing the book; to Margaret Dellinger and Don Hankinson for the cover design; to Marion Radeer for invaluable clerical assistance; and to numerous others, not identified here, who contributed significantly to the review process and who advised, encouraged, and supported their efforts.

To integrate the quality improvement concepts outlined in the *AT&T Quality Improvement Cycle* with these process quality management and improvement guidelines, the AT&T Quality Steering Committee chartered the following work group to develop *Process Quality Management and Improvement Guidelines* (Issue 1.1):

> Roberta Coleman, Chairman   John MacDorman
> Susan Annitto   Elaine Piskorik
> Joe Crupi   Greg Shaw
> Steve Holt

CONTENTS

P • A • R • T   O • N • E

OVERVIEW

"They began running when they liked and left off when they liked, so that it was not easy to know when the race was over."

The Caucus Race

The animals were all thoroughly wet after Alice's burst of tears, and a race seemed the best way for everyone to get dry. But how could anyone win the race, Alice wondered, if they didn't all run to the same place?

Many processes, and especially those that have evolved and adapted over time, may bear some resemblance to the caucus race: everyone running hard but without, perhaps, a clear sense of direction, an understanding of what is driving the process.

Part One provides an overview of a methodology to help focus process management efforts, to get everyone moving in the same direction toward the same goals.

INTRODUCTION

"It sounded an excellent plan, no doubt, and very neatly and simply arranged. The only difficulty was, she had not the smallest idea how to set about it..."

Alice

Purpose of this guide

The puzzle of *how to set about it* has stalled many an excellent plan. These guidelines offer a proven method for setting about managing and improving process quality. These guidelines are based on the premise that all work can be defined as a process and that everyone manages a process. The guidelines are intended to help you fulfill the AT&T Quality Policy directives of ensuring customer satisfaction and optimal use of resources as you

- manage and improve the performance of existing processes

- design new processes.

The impetus for developing these guidelines was the recognition of the need for a structured approach to managing and improving the quality of service and administrative functions. However, the underlying principles have proven to be applicable to *any* process, including manufacturing, design, and development processes.

This book is one of a series of publications that support the implementation of an integrated AT&T Quality System. Your process management responsibilities may include working with quality improvement teams. The *AT&T Quality Improvement Cycle*[1] (QIC) offers guidelines for teams working on specific problems and opportunities within a process.

Benefits of the methodology

The disciplined application of the entire methodology leads to sustained process quality improvement. Benefits of this application include:

- Reduced firefighting (crisis management)

- Clarification of work priorities

- Better coordination among the major groups working within the organization

- Systematic identification and removal of the *root cause* or basis of problems

- Prevention of problems

- Decision-making based on facts

- Achievement of quality objectives in less time, with less rework.

Using the guidelines

This is a book of guidelines, not rules. The methodology is a roadmap for achieving sustained process quality improvement. To realize the benefits of the methodology, the guidelines must be applied with sound management judgement at all stages of your work function.

These guidelines assume that you have identified a process for management and improvement. In many cases, this is established by defined job responsibilities. In other cases, however—especially in high-level processes—some effort is required to select the critical end-to-end processes that affect end-customer needs and internal business objectives.

To apply these guidelines requires an understanding of what quality is and why it is important. To implement the methodology also requires some familiarity with basic quality tools such as control charts, flowcharts, and Pareto diagrams.

Organization of this guide

- **Part One, Overview**, begins with this **Introduction**, establishing the purpose of the guidelines and defining terms in the context of the guidelines. The next section, **The Quality Environment**, relates the methodology to the customer-supplier relationship and the AT&T Quality Architecture. The third section, **The Methodology**, describes process quality management and improvement in terms of the general principles behind the methodology and the purpose of each of its seven steps.

- **Part Two, Management & Improvement Steps**, includes one section for each of the seven steps in the methodology, describing activities and tasks to be performed at each step with references to available tools to help implement each step. A continuing example throughout **Part Two** illustrates the application of the methodology at each step. The last section in **Part Two** features a chart summarizing the steps in process management and improvement.

- The **Appendix** is a dictionary of tools recommended in the methodology.

- A **Glossary of Terms** and a **Reference List** of source and supplementary publications follow the Appendix.

Definitions   As used in these guidelines:

Quality means consistently meeting customer expectations. A key internal objective is to assure that business objectives are also satisfied.

A *process* is a set of interrelated work activities that are characterized by a set of specific inputs and value-added tasks that produce a set of specific outputs. A process can be contained within a functional organization, or it can span several functional organizations. (Examples of processes include service provisioning, document production/distribution, circuit pack manufacturing, service restoration, and customer complaint resolution.)

Processes may consist of a collection of *subprocesses*. For example, the service provisioning process includes a number of subprocesses such as service engineering, installation of service, and order writing.

Process performance refers to how effectively and efficiently a process satisfies customer requirements.

Process quality management means planning and executing the regular activities necessary to sustain process performance and identify opportunities for improving customer satisfaction and reducing costs.

Process quality improvement means acting on opportunities to drive the process to a new level of performance.

A *functional organization* is an organization responsible for one of the major corporate business functions, for example, marketing, sales, design, manufacturing, or distribution.

Customer refers to the recipient or beneficiary of the outputs of the process work efforts or the purchaser of its products and services. The customer may be either internal or external to the company.

Supplier refers to individuals or groups who provide inputs to the process. Suppliers can be internal or external to a company, group, or organization.

THE QUALITY ENVIRONMENT

"'I don't think they play at all fairly,' Alice began, in a rather complaining tone... 'they don't seem to have any rules in particular. At least if there are, nobody attends to them.'"

The foundation

Rules alone do not guarantee success, but the absence of established and defined principles or the lack of commitment to them almost certainly guarantees failure. AT&T's Quality Policy defines one overriding principle in support of a corporate quality environment, challenging us to "consistently provide products and services that meet the quality expectations of our customers." Managers and employees are encouraged to meet this challenge by focusing work efforts on improving customer satisfaction and operating processes more efficiently.

This challenge applies at every functional level of business—everyone has customers and suppliers. Effective process quality management demands that customer requirements guide day-to-day work activities. Using a customer-driven approach to quality management ensures that the outputs of your job satisfy your customer and that the process is responsive to changes in customer needs.

AT&T's customer/supplier model is a graphical depiction of this business strategy. This model is the *foundation* of the process quality management and improvement methodology, providing a framework for establishing and maintaining effective relations with customers and suppliers. The model begins with customer requirements and stresses active measures of customer satisfaction to provide ongoing feedback for process improvement. The model is constructed on the premise that each of us has customers—either inside or outside the company—who use the outputs of our job and suppliers who provide inputs to our job.

Customer/ supplier model

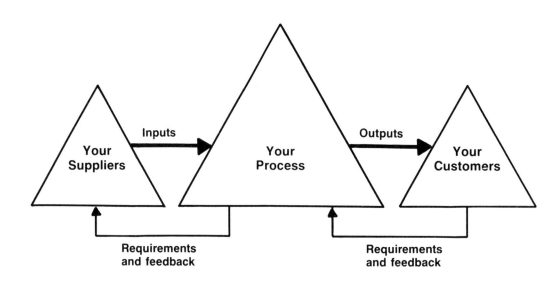

This figure illustrates how requirements and feedback drive the process as it converts supplier inputs into outputs delivered to customers.

The AT&T Quality Architecture

The process quality management and improvement methodology supports an overall corporate quality architecture, a plan for building an effective corporate management system with *quality* as its foundation. Within the architecture, quality-related activities are linked across the boundaries of major functional organizations, such as marketing, sales, design, manufacturing, and distribution. Functional organizations are linked to one another through customer/supplier relationships and are driven by end-customer quality requirements as well as internal business objectives. Through this model, work groups are linked within functional organizations and employees are linked within work groups.

The AT&T Quality Architecture supports the AT&T Business Plan, which outlines AT&T's business and strategic direction. A principal requirement set forth in the Business Plan is that, at the level of each functional organization, a quality management system must be in place to:

- Interpret and communicate the AT&T Quality Policy
- Guide the establishment of a quality environment in terms of human resources, management, information, and facilities
- Establish priorities
- Set goals and follow up on results
- Resolve issues
- Allocate resources
- Provide staffing and training
- Provide rewards/recognition
- Identify processes and subprocesses having direct impact on customer and business needs.

THE METHODOLOGY

"'Digging for apples, yer honour!'
'Digging for apples, indeed!' said the Rabbit angrily."

Overview of the methodology

Digging, no matter how deep the hole or fine the equipment, will never produce apples; it's the wrong way to go about it. The idea of *digging for apples* captures all the different kinds of misunderstanding and confusion that can undermine a process. The process quality management and improvement methodology offers a structured approach to defining your process goals and understanding the *best way to go about achieving them*. The methodology synthesizes quality management practices that have proven effective inside and outside of AT&T.

The following principles have guided the development of the methodology:

- Process quality improvement focuses on the end-to-end process.

- The mindset of quality is one of prevention and continuous improvement.

- Everyone manages a process at some level and is simultaneously a customer and a supplier.

- Customer needs drive process quality improvement.

- Corrective action focuses on removing the root cause of the problem rather than on treating its symptoms.

- Process simplification reduces opportunities for errors and rework.

- Process quality improvement results from a disciplined and structured application of the quality management principles.

The cycle   The methodology is a two-phase cycle: you *manage* the process and *improve* the process, and continuously repeat the cycle. The following figure illustrates the cyclical nature of the methodology.

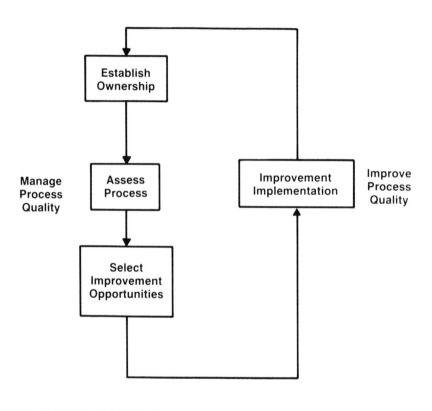

Design of the methodology	The methodology includes tasks to be performed at each of four distinct stages within these management and improvement phases. Each stage has a specific purpose:

Stage	Purpose
Ownership	To ensure that someone is in charge of the process and that a team exists to carry out day-to-day quality management activities.
Assessment	To assure that the process is clearly defined, that customer expectations are clearly understood, and that measures are in place to determine how well the process is satisfying customer requirements and internal business objectives.
Opportunity Selection	To understand how internal process problems affect customer satisfaction and cost and to identify and rank order opportunities for process improvement.
Improvement	To achieve and sustain a new level of process performance by implementing an action plan for realizing opportunities identified in the previous stage.

The following discussion identifies the main objectives of each of the four stages of the methodology, indicating the logical steps in which these objectives are realized. **Part Two** offers a detailed discussion of each step, its associated objectives, tools, and activities.

Ownership stage	The objectives of this stage are:

- To identify an overall process owner who is ultimately accountable for the process and who can manage the process across functional or organizational boundaries (**Step 1**).
- To establish a process management team that, ideally, represents management/ownership of major constituent subprocesses of the cross-functional process (**Step 1**).
- To define roles and responsibilities of the team and ensure that everyone involved in the application of process quality management and improvement has personal ownership of process performance (**Step 1**).

Assessment stage	The objectives of this stage are: • To understand how the process operates (**Step 2**) • To identify customer needs in measurable terms (**Step 2**) • To determine what elements of the process should be measured and controlled to meet customer requirements (**Step 3**) • To test and then implement appropriate new measures or validate existing measures on a wide scale (**Step 3**) • To gather data on process performance (**Step 4**) • To control and stabilize process performance (**Step 4**) • To assess process performance against customer requirements (**Step 4**).
Opportunity selection stage	The objectives of this stage are: • To identify critical internal process problems that are affecting customer satisfaction and cost (**Step 5**) • To identify process simplification opportunities (**Step 5**) • To rank improvement opportunities based on customer satisfaction and business objectives (**Step 6**) • To set appropriate quality improvement and performance targets (**Step 6**) • To identify quality improvement projects to pursue (**Step 6**).
Improvement stage	The objectives of this stage are: • To organize a quality improvement team that will develop an action plan to address opportunities for process quality improvement (**Step 7**) • To determine and remove root causes of problems (**Step 7**) • To control and monitor the process at the improved level of performance (**Step 7**) • To monitor and assess process performance on an ongoing basis (**Step 7**).

**Relation-
ship of
steps**

The following table illustrates relationships between the phases, stages, and the steps in the methodology. Because the methodology is iterative and flexible, additional relationships exist in individual implementations.

Phases	Stages	Steps	
MANAGEMENT	Ownership	1.	Establish Process Management Responsibilities
	Assessment	2.	Define Process and Identify Customer Requirements
		3.	Define and Establish Measures
		4.	Assess Conformance to Customer Requirements
	Opportunity Selection	5.	Investigate Process to Identify Improvement Opportunities
		6.	Rank Improvement Opportunities and Set Objectives
IMPROVEMENT	Improvement	7.	Improve Process Quality

**Applying
the
method-
ology**

Sustained process quality improvement requires the disciplined application of the entire methodology. By focusing on the entire process—understanding its boundaries, interfaces, customers, suppliers, and capabilities and assessing its performance—you can make a more informed decision about how best to achieve and maintain improved process performance.

The methodology should not be viewed as a rigid process: It is often useful to revisit an earlier step, for example, as you carry out the implementation of the methodology. Generally, **Steps 1** through **6** need to be completed to identify opportunities for bringing your process to a new level of performance. However, opportunities for immediate improvement may become obvious as you complete individual steps. Corrective actions should be carried out at these points, as deemed appropriate by the process manager and process management team.

P · A · R · T T · W · O

MANAGEMENT & IMPROVEMENT STEPS

"It's always six o'clock now... It's always tea-time"

The March Hare

Time stood still for the Mad Hatter and the March Hare, and they quite enjoyed their endless tea party. But time never stops in today's competitive business environment. The process that worked yesterday may no longer satisfy the requirements of today's customers; it may not make the best use of today's resources. And today's methods and procedures will very likely not be effective in tomorrow's world.

The seven steps described in **Part Two** will help you:

- to understand your process from beginning to end, its customers, their expectations, and the elements of the process that contribute to or hinder the realization of those expectations;

- to continuously evaluate and improve your process from that perspective;

- to keep your process current and responsive to changes in customer requirements and to technological advances that may contribute to internal efficiencies.

17

MANAGEMENT & IMPROVEMENT STEPS

Step 1:   Establish Process Management Responsibilities

Step 2:   Define Process and Identify Customer Requirements

Step 3:   Define and Establish Measures

Step 4:   Assess Conformance to Customer Requirements

Step 5:   Investigate Process to Identify Improvement
          Opportunities

Step 6:   Rank Improvement Opportunities and Set Objectives

Step 7:   Improve Process Quality

STEP 1: ESTABLISH PROCESS MANAGEMENT RESPONSIBILITIES

"'Who are you?' said the Caterpillar."

Overview

Understanding *who* you are—in the context of the whole process—is the first step toward understanding the process. It is a question that must be answered for each participant in the process as the basis for clarifying responsibilities and assigning accountability. Process quality management and improvement begins by establishing and communicating clearly defined responsibilities for the ongoing operation of the process. Two concepts are central to the theme of establishing process management responsibilities:

- The *Process Owner*: ownership rests with a single individual[2] who coordinates the multiple functions of a process, designates the process management team, and is ultimately accountable for the effectiveness of a process.

- The *Process Management Team*: the individuals appointed to execute the process management steps and provide the focus for continuous quality improvement.

Ideally, these individuals have management responsibility for the major subprocesses that make up the process. Assigning ultimate accountability for the process focuses attention on *resolving process problems*, as opposed to ascribing blame.

Objectives of this section

This section provides guidelines for:

- Defining the roles and responsibilities that support the application of process quality management and improvement

- Defining the responsibilities unique to the process owner

- Defining criteria for process ownership.

Process owner responsibilities

The process owner is ultimately accountable for overall process performance and must coordinate all process functions to ensure cost-effective customer satisfaction. Process owner responsibilities include:

- Organizing the process management team, as appropriate, and communicating their roles and responsibilities
- Measuring and tracking progress
- Establishing and maintaining process control
- Resolving/escalating process issues
- Documenting the process
- Initiating process reviews
- Allocating resources.

Depending on the level of the process, the process owner may need to appoint a process management team to help implement the process management and improvement steps. This is especially true for high-level processes that span many work functions.

Criteria for process ownership

Recommended criteria for process ownership include:

- Responsibility for process results
- Authority or ability to effect changes
- Ability to carry out process owner's responsibilities
- Understanding of the process end-to-end.

This list is not exhaustive; you may need to add criteria to reflect your process needs. Generally, process ownership results from defined job responsibilities. However, in complex, high-level processes, it is not always readily apparent who is the process owner. In these cases, ownership is typically assigned by executive decision. The authority and resources to resolve any process issues must accompany the assignment of process ownership.

Process management team responsibilities	The process management team includes representatives from each major work function within the process. The team members' responsibilities include: • Identifying and organizing key implementors to carry out the process management steps • Identifying quality improvement projects • Designating and supporting quality improvement teams • Creating an environment in which all process participants can contribute to process improvement.
Roles and responsibilities	Unanimous commitment to process improvement is essential to achieve the overall process objectives, commitment from *everyone* who works in the process—process participants, as well as members of the process management team. Everyone who works in a process should: • Understand and practice the principles of the customer/supplier model • Identify and communicate potential process improvements to the process management team • Express a willingness to participate in quality improvement teams. The roles and responsibilities of individual process members are dictated by the scope of the process. For instance, a line manager may have operational duties within the context of a high-level process, but will have all the responsibilities of a process owner for the management and improvement of his or her operation.
Example	A Document Production Center produces and distributes standardized reports upon receipt of handwritten material. The process cuts across three work functions: Production Coordination, Reproduction, and Text Processing. In this example, a single person is in charge of each of the major work functions. The Center Manager assumes the role of process owner. Responsibilities include managing the interfunctional interfaces and ensuring that the functional units work together to achieve the overall process objectives. The Text Processing Supervisor, Reproduction Supervisor, and Production Coordinator make up the process management team in support of the Center Manager.

Each member of the Document Production Center assumes ownership for the particular subset of activities that constitutes his or her job.

Throughout **Part Two**, this document production and distribution process example illustrates the application of each step of the methodology.

___

STEP 2: DEFINE PROCESS AND IDENTIFY CUSTOMER REQUIREMENTS

"I heard the Queen say only yesterday you deserve to be beheaded... It was for bringing the cook tulip roots instead of onions."

Five of Spades

Overview

Tulip roots are prized by the gardener, but they're not very useful to the cook. When the customer is preparing dinner, onions are better than tulip roots—illustrating how important it is to understand *the customer's requirements for process output*.

The activities in **Step 2** help to focus the efforts of the process management team and to ensure that all members share a common understanding of the process and its requirements. There are two elements to this step:

- *Defining the process* means to describe its boundaries, inputs, outputs, suppliers, customers, and major activities/subprocesses. This exercise helps you understand how the process *actually* operates, including interactions with customers, suppliers, and between major groups. This step must involve those who actually perform the work.

- *Identifying customer requirements* enables you to establish specific and measurable customer needs. These customer requirements, together with business objectives, drive the process requirements that you communicate to *your* suppliers.

Objectives of this section

This section provides guidelines for:

- Defining your process in terms of its boundaries and interfaces

- Developing a clear picture of how your process operates

- Documenting process work-flows at a high level

- Capturing and quantifying customer requirements so that process quality management and improvement activities are properly driven.

Defining the Process

Goals   You can select from several different methods to define your process. Your chosen method should help you to:

- Focus on the interfaces between work groups
- Inventory inputs, outputs, suppliers, customers, and the activities of work groups
- Understand how work activities are interconnected
- Move on to more detailed flowcharting.

Method   The table [3] below describes a method that has proven helpful for describing how a process actually operates, including interactions with customers, suppliers, and between major work groups. Note that the example and figures cited in this table follow the table, but are *not* extracted from Reference 3.

Activity	Tasks	Tools*
1. Define process boundaries and major groups.†	• Define the purpose. • Define the process boundaries as follows: — The process begins with ... — The process ends with ... • List the major groups contained within the process and draw a box with as many columns. Label the top of each column with a group name.‡ See Figure 1, page 26 for example.	• Interview
2. Identify process outputs and customers.	• List all the outputs the process produces to the right of the process box. • List all the customers, that is, recipients of process output, to the right of the output list. • As a check, ask yourself: — For each output: Are we leaving any customers out? — For each customer: Do they receive any additional outputs from us? See Figure 2, page 27 for example.	• Interview • Q-MAP

* See the **Appendix** for descriptions of the tools.

† Groups describe the process' internal boundaries. Depending on the level of the process, groups may be organizational units, functions, departments, work groups, etc.

‡ Unless you are working with a high-level process, a process box that includes more than five groups is probably too detailed.

Activity	Tasks	Tools

3. Identify process inputs and suppliers.	• List all the inputs the process receives to the left of the process box.
	• List all the suppliers of process input to the left of the input list.
	• As a check, ask yourself:
	  — For each input: Are we leaving any suppliers out?
	  — For each supplier: Do they provide us any additional inputs?
	
	See Figure 3, page 27 for example.
		• Interview
		• Q-MAP

4. Identify sub-processes and flows.	• For each input listed, define the work activity that it feeds. (Note that work activities include both those performed by people as well as those performed by automated support systems.) Draw and label a representative activity box in the appropriate column.* • For each activity defined, ask what outputs it produces, what activities it feeds, and who performs the activity. Interview the people who actually perform the work. • Label the new activity boxes and continue generating work/information flows and work activities until you connect into all process outputs defined to the right of the process box.† See Figure 4, page 28 for example.	• Block Diagram • Interview

5. Validate the process definition.	• Perform the following checks:
	  — Do all the work/information flows properly map into process inputs and outputs?
	  — Have you captured, within the context of this process box, all the potential paths work/information can take, including rework loops, ad-hoc procedures, and work-arounds?
	  — Does your diagram represent what really happens, not how you think things should be or how they were originally designed?
	
	The final diagram should be a record of how the current process actually operates. It may take several passes to get the diagram right.
	• Date the diagram and keep this record up to date as part of managing process change.	

* Remember that process flows are documented at a *high level*; avoid details. The only symbols used are activity boxes representing subprocesses and arrows representing intermediate inputs/outputs between activities. The activities should not be so broad as to run across groups/columns. More than three activity boxes in series in a column with no outside inputs probably indicates too much detail.

† For a complex process, it may be best to inventory the activities of each major group first and make the interconnections.

Example

Figures 1 through 4 illustrate the creation of a process box for the document production and distribution process.

Define boundaries and major groups

Figure 1 shows:

- The process boundaries: the process begins with the receipt of handwritten material, and the process ends with the distribution of standardized reports.

- The major groups contained within the process: Production Coordination, Reproduction, and Text Processing. Each column in the process box is labeled with a group name.

Figure 1

Statement of purpose: The purpose of the process is to produce and distribute standardized reports upon receipt of handwritten material.

The process begins with the receipt of handwritten material.

Production Coordination	Reproduction	Text Processing

The process ends with the distribution of standardized reports.

*Identify
outputs and
customers*

Figure 2 shows:

- The outputs of the process (standardized reports) listed to the right of the process box
- The customer (upper level management) listed to the right of the output.

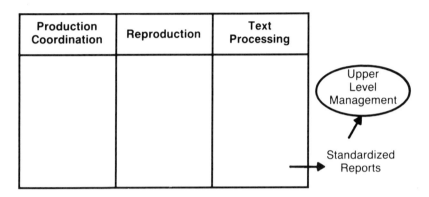

Figure 2

*Identify
inputs and
suppliers*

Figure 3 shows:

- The inputs to the process (handwritten material) listed to the left of the process box
- The suppliers of the inputs (writers) listed to the left of the inputs.

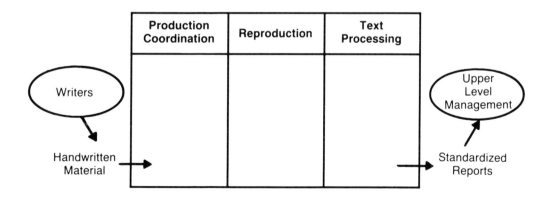

Figure 3

Identify subprocesses and flows

Figure 4 shows:

- The work activity that is fed by inputs to the process. For example, the input "Handwritten Material" is fed into the activity "Receive Handwritten Document," which is performed by the Production Coordination Group.

- The output flows between activities. For example, the activity "Enter into Word Processor" produces a printed document that feeds the activity "Review/Edit/ Assemble Document," which is performed by the Production Coordination Group.

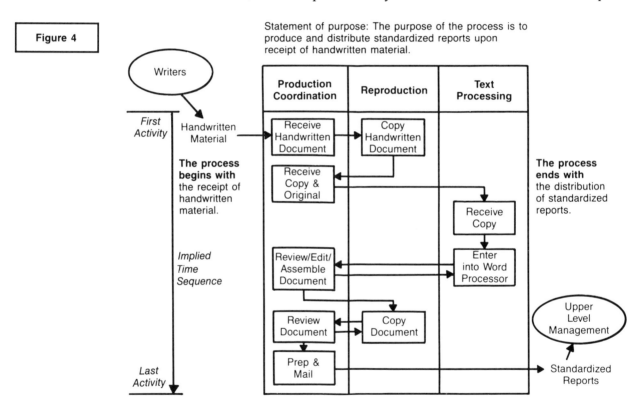

Figure 4

Statement of purpose: The purpose of the process is to produce and distribute standardized reports upon receipt of handwritten material.

Validate definition

The last activity in process definition is to validate the diagram and keep it up to date. Tracking sample documents through the sequence of work activities confirms that the diagram accurately represents the current process.

Identifying Customer Requirements

Focus
Customer requirements are the primary driving force directing process quality management and improvement. If you have sufficient resources, you should, of course, address all of your customer's quality needs at once. If you do not have the resources to address *all* customer needs immediately, identify the most *critical* needs. After addressing the most critical needs, you can focus on your customer's less critical needs.

Method
The following table lists activities and tasks to identify and assign priorities to customer requirements.

Activity	Tasks	Tools

1. Conduct customer needs analysis.*	• Understand how your customers use your output.
	• Identify most critical outputs.
	  — Work with your customers to identify those things needed from you to do their job right the first time.
	• Identify most critical quality characteristics of each output.
	  — Work with your customers to identify the characteristics of the output that are particularly important to them, for example, timeliness, completeness, accuracy, and format.
	• Define measurable needs. Work with your customer to define:
	  — Quality characteristics in specific and measurable terms.
	  — The target representing satisfaction associated with each measurable need.
	• Have your customer rank the measurable needs in order of importance.
	• If you have more than one customer, develop a single rank-ordered list of all your customers' needs.
		• Affinity Diagram
		• Customer-Needs Analysis
		• Customer/Supplier Questionnaire
		• Interview
		• Q-MAP
		• Survey
		• Tree Diagram

* To facilitate customer needs analysis, it may be necessary to use an example that illustrates the major tasks and results of this activity.

Activity	Tasks	Tools
2. Define requirements.	• Perform benchmarking, if appropriate.* • Formulate requirements based on measurable customer needs identified in Activity 1 and on benchmarks, where applicable. • Confirm requirement definition with customer. • Document customer requirements, including the output, quality characteristics, unit of measure, and target. • Define subprocess requirements and communicate your own requirements to your suppliers.	• Benchmarking • Q-MAP

Example

The Document Production Center process management team uses customer needs analysis and benchmarking to identify its customer requirements.

Conduct needs analysis

The process management team interviews a cross-section of the upper level managers who receive the standardized reports. From a list of possible needs—including turnaround time, copy quality, accuracy, and special handling—managers are asked to select those needs that they view as most critical.

A majority of the managers rank accuracy and turnaround time as their most critical needs: All managers express the need for no errors and a 3- to 5-day turnaround time.

Define requirements

As a result of customer needs analysis, the process management team decides to benchmark turnaround time and number of errors. They obtain market research data on Company D, a direct competitor, and Company N, a noncompetitor, and discover that both companies can process similar documents in three days with no errors.

Based on customer needs analysis and market research data, the process management team defines and documents the following customer requirements in terms of output, quality characteristics, unit of measure, and target. These requirements are represented in the following table.

* See the **Appendix** for a detailed description of this tool.

	Output	Quality Characteristics	Unit of Measure	Performance Target
Customer Requirement #1	Standardized Report	Accuracy	Number of Errors	0 Errors
Customer Requirement #2		Timeliness	End-to-End Processing Time in Days	3 Days

The process management team also defines and communicates the following supplier requirements in terms of output, quality characteristics, unit of measure, and performance target. These requirements are represented in the following table.

	Output	Quality Characteristics	Unit of Measure	Performance Target
Supplier Requirement #1	Handwritten Document	Timeliness	Time Document Submitted	Before 10 a.m.
Supplier Requirement #2	Document Production Request Form	Completeness	Percent of Fields Completed	100%

STEP 3:   DEFINE AND ESTABLISH MEASURES

"... yes, that's about the right distance—but then I wonder what Latitude or Longitude I've got to?"

Alice

Overview

The *right measures* are critical to the effective management of work processes: measures that give you specific and useful information such as Alice needed— information about degree and direction, as well as quantity. The right measures provide the basis for determining how well you and your suppliers are meeting requirements and how close you are to your target, and for monitoring progress with respect to requirements. In addition, measures are used to:

- Track accomplishment of the goals set by an organization, group, or individual.

- Recognize when improvement is made or is required.

- Track the use of resources and assess how efficiently these resources are being used to provide products and services to customers.

- Provide information that supports decisions to improve the process.

If you cannot measure your results, then you cannot control your process and improve your performance. You must develop and install:

- Overall measures to gauge customer satisfaction.

- In-process measures and decision points at which you will take action to assure conformance to customer requirements. In-process measures generally focus on internal efficiency and respond to business objectives as well as customer requirements.

- Measures for input quality from suppliers.

- Satisfaction feedback system.

Objectives of this section

This section provides guidelines for:

- Translating customer requirements into effective measures

- Understanding when and how to establish new measures.

33

Characteristics of effective measures	The effectiveness of a measure of quality can be evaluated by the degree to which it is: • Related to customer requirements • Practical to implement • Easy to understand • Able to drive desired behavior • Developed with inputs from and consensus with work groups • Specific.

Establishing measures

To establish effective measures, perform the activities and tasks in the following table.

Activity	Tasks	Tools
1. Review customer requirements.	• Review customer requirements and subprocess requirements, as determined in **Step 2**.	• Q-MAP
2. Determine effective measures.	• Review characteristics of effective measures. • Brainstorm potential measures and rank order them.	• Brainstorming • Multivoting • Nominal Group Technique • Q-MAP
3. Review and validate existing measures against requirements and criteria.	• Determine if existing measures are appropriate according to customer requirements. • Check the measures against characteristics noted above.	• Q-MAP
4. Install new measures (as appropriate).	• Test new measures to assess effectiveness. • Make appropriate changes to measures. • Implement new measures on wide scale.	• Q-MAP

Activity	Tasks	Tools
5. Implement reporting system.	• Assign responsibility for data collection and reporting. • Determine report recipients (process owner, functional managers, people working in the process). • Determine frequency and content of report. — Frequency: as frequently as necessary to ensure prompt corrective action. — Content: individual results, trends, rank-ordered list of contributing factors.	• Q-MAP
6. Establish satisfaction feedback system with customers and suppliers.	• Design satisfaction response method that is keyed to specific requirements. • Determine method and frequency of response. • Establish commitment. — Customer will provide ongoing satisfaction feedback. — Supplier will be responsive to customer feedback.	• Interview • Q-MAP • Survey

Example The process management team takes the following steps to define and establish measures of process quality.

Review requirements In **Step 2**, the process management team documented the following requirements for achieving customer satisfaction:

• Documents are delivered to the customer within three days of receipt of handwritten material

• Documents are accurate (no errors, such as pages out of sequence, wrong information).

Determine effective measures After reviewing characteristics of effective measures, the process management team decides on measures that will accurately reflect the performance of the process as it relates to customer and supplier requirements:

• Number of days from receipt of handwritten material to delivery of final document

• Percentage of documents with one or more errors

- Number of errors in document by error type
- Percent of document production requests—handwritten document and document production request forms—returned to supplier.

Review current measures

The measure currently in place tracks the number of documents distributed each month. While this measure is useful to track resource requirements, it does not reflect customer requirements. Additional measures need to be installed to evaluate the quality of the documents.

Install new measures

After evaluating the data collected from Reproduction, Text Processing, and Production Coordination during a two-month trial, the Center Manager implements the new measures.

Implement reporting system

The Production Coordinator is assigned responsibility for data collection and establishes the following reporting system:

- Data showing progress toward customer requirements will be collected and reported on a monthly basis. This monthly progress report will be sent to the Reproduction Supervisor and the Text Processing Supervisor, with a copy to the Center Manager.
- The progress report will include a summary of current results and historical trends.

Establish feedback

To gain ongoing, objective feedback on the process, the supervisors and manager jointly agree with their customers that every three months the center will: 1) contact the customer for feedback and 2) report on feedback. In addition, the process management team agrees to provide suppliers monthly feedback on the percent of document production requests returned to suppliers because forms are incomplete.

STEP 4: ASSESS CONFORMANCE TO CUSTOMER REQUIREMENTS

"'It doesn't prove anything of the sort!' said Alice."

Overview

With measures in place to track the key elements of your process, you can gather useful data about how your process is working. But measures alone cannot *prove* the effectiveness of your process. It is only when you analyze that data from the perspective of your customer's requirements that you really begin to know how *well* your process is working, that is, how well process outputs conform to customer requirements.

This assessment should always include a measurement of customer satisfaction. In addition, the assessment should use quantitative data to formally track process performance against requirements. Monitoring the process performance with respect to customer requirements enables the process manager to identify gaps between *process capability*—what a process can be expected to do over the long run—and what represents 100 percent customer satisfaction. Identification of these gaps in performance, in conjunction with customer satisfaction feedback, provides the basis for process improvement efforts.

A number of different methods can be used to assess conformance to customer requirements. These methods vary depending on the frequency of process outputs. If your process has *frequent* outputs, then statistical process control (SPC) methods are useful for assessing conformance to requirements. Examples of such processes include order processing, reproduction and distribution, and product manufacturing.

Statistical process control may also be useful with processes having *infrequent* outputs if the SPC methods can be applied to internal subprocesses that have frequent outputs. Examples of processes with *infrequent outputs* include market research, annual business planning, and methods and procedures development.

Objectives of this section

This section provides guidelines for:

- Assessing the process performance
- Using statistical methods to control the quality of process output.

Assessing conformance: frequent outputs

To assess conformance to requirements for processes with *frequent* outputs, perform the activities and tasks in the following table.

Activity	Tasks	Tools
1. Collect and review measurement data on process outputs.	• Review customer satisfaction measurement results to find out if process performance conforms to their requirements. Determine if problems are sporadic or chronic. • Collect quantitative data on process performance as it relates directly to customer requirements. Construct control charts* of data to identify and measure process variability.	• Control Chart • Interview • Q-MAP • Survey
2. Identify and remove any causes of abnormal variation.	• Analyze control charts to determine whether abnormal variation† in process performance exists. • If abnormal variation exists: — Develop and test theories of what is causing the abnormal variation. — Decide on the few vital causes. — Develop and test alternative solutions. — Implement solutions that will solve the most significant causes of abnormal variation and bring process into control. • Monitor process to ensure that it remains stable.	• Brainstorming • Cause and Effect Diagram • Control Chart • Multivoting • Nominal Group Technique • Pareto Diagram
3. Compare performance of the stable process to requirements and determine chronic problem areas.	• Talk to customers or review customer satisfaction measurement results and compare performance level of the stable process to requirements. • Compare quantitative performance data to customer requirements and determine if gaps exist. • Document findings and continue to monitor process performance and customer satisfaction. If the stable process meets customer requirements, continued monitoring is essential for maintaining process stability. • Go to **Step 5, Investigate Process to Identify Improvement Opportunities**. Even if your process is stable and is capable of meeting requirements, you can continuously improve your process.	• Control Chart

* See the **Appendix**, for a detailed description of this tool.

† *Abnormal variations* are changes that cannot be accounted for by typical day-to-day variation in process performance.

Assessing conformance: infrequent outputs

To assess conformance to requirements for processes with *infrequent* outputs, perform the activities and tasks in the following table.

Activity	Tasks	Tools
1. Collect and review measurement data on process outputs.	• Review customer satisfaction measurement results to find out if process performance conforms to their requirements. • Collect quantitative data on process performance as it relates directly to customer requirements.	• Interview • Q-MAP • Survey
2. Compare process output performance to requirements and determine chronic problem areas.	• Compare quantitative performance data to customer requirements and determine if gaps exist. • Document findings and continue to monitor process performance and customer satisfaction. • Go to **Step 5, Investigate Process to Identify Improvement Opportunities**. Even if your process is stable and is capable of meeting requirements, you can continuously improve your process.	• Graph • Q-MAP

Example

The document production and distribution process is an example of a process with frequent outputs. The process management team takes the following steps to assess the process' conformance to customer requirements.

Collect and review measurement data

From data collected in follow-up contact with the customers (report recipients) the Reproduction Supervisor learns:

• that the center has not been consistently meeting the customer requirements established in **Step 2** for a 3-day delivery interval (from receipt of handwritten material to delivery of the final document)

• that recently the document delivery interval has lengthened dramatically, indicating abnormal variation.

This data is plotted on an X-bar control chart,* illustrated below.

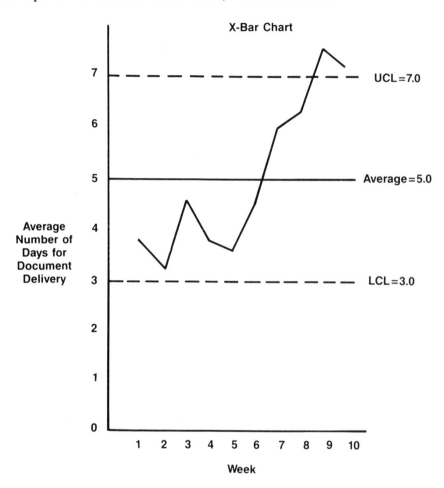

Remove
abnormal
variation

From possible reasons for the increase in the delivery interval, the cause is traced to the database used for generating mailing labels: While distribution lists for documents are continually updated, the database is not. Establishing a system for updating the database resolves the problem of the abnormally long delivery interval and reduces overall variation.

---

* For proper analysis, an X-Bar chart should be accompanied by an R chart. In this example, only the X-Bar chart is shown.

*Determine
chronic
problems*

After the mailing database is updated, results are plotted on control charts. The measurement indicates that the process is still unable to consistently meet the 3-day requirement. (See the **Appendix** for more information on control charts.)

The following X-bar chart shows a normal variation in process performance. However, if you compare the long-term delivery interval (average of 3.7) to the customer requirement of three days, you can see that, although the process is in control, it is not capable of meeting customer requirements consistently. This indicates that the process needs to be changed.

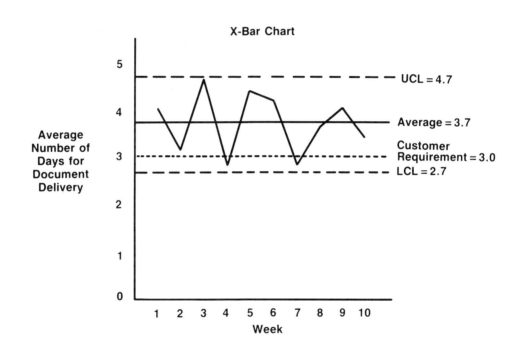

STEP 5: INVESTIGATE PROCESS TO IDENTIFY IMPROVEMENT OPPORTUNITIES

"The Queen had only one way of settling all difficulties, great or small.
'Off with his head!' she said without even looking around."

Overview

A reflexive reaction like the Queen's is often the least effective solution to a problem. Investigating the process to identify and better understand the sources of difficulty is essential to eliminating process problems that affect output quality.

This step is used to identify the specific internal process problems that influence customer satisfaction and costs. To evaluate the current process operation from this perspective, you must ask yourself whether there is a better way of doing things and what internal changes could have the greatest positive impact on the quality of process output. A systematic investigation of the process often reveals significant improvement opportunities, including process simplification.

This step integrates process flow charting and data analysis. Internal process problems are identified by gaining a more detailed understanding of how the process actually operates.

Objectives of this section

This section provides guidelines for:

- Identifying the critical internal process problems impacting customer satisfaction and costs

- Identifying process simplification opportunities.

Investigating your process

To investigate your process, perform the activities and tasks in the following table.

Activity	Tasks	Tools
1. Gather data on process problems.	• Identify the critical problems with process output as evidenced by the result of assessment in **Step 4** or the inability of the process to meet business objectives. • Identify and talk with the people who do the work to obtain information on internal process problems linked to output deficiencies. Use the diagram produced in **Step 2**, as a means to focus discussions on: — sources of error — simplification opportunities (See Checklist 1, page 45) — interactions at interfaces, such as, what happens to intermediate products between activities (See Checklist 2, page 45) — bottlenecks — the absence of adequate internal controls, including the administration of process change. • Gather measurable data to further investigate/validate and baseline internal process performance. Such data often includes: — error rates per activity — throughput and processing time per activity — rework and scrap per activity.	• Brainstorming • Interview • Multivoting
2. Identify potential process problems to pursue.	• Evaluate data to identify the potential internal process problems impacting customer satisfaction and costs. List these problems. • Review list of potential internal process problems and decide which of these require further investigation or clarification. • Segment the problems requiring further investigation into two lists: — problems that require additional data at the same level (go back to Activity 1) — problems to investigate in more detail (continue to Activity 3).	• Nominal Group Technique • Pareto Diagram
3. Document potential problem areas.	• Determine what activity or group of activities to investigate in detail. • Create flow diagram* of problem areas using the conventions described in the **Appendix**. • Produce written description.†	• Flowchart

* Validate by tracking work and information through the process. Date it and record subsequent changes.

† Document key information not covered by process flow diagrams, for example, remote locations, sensitive interfaces, etc.

Activity	Tasks	Tools
4. Gather data on subprocess problems.	These tasks are similar to the tasks described under Activity 1, but are applied at the subprocess level of investigation. Use the documentation developed in Activity 3 to help focus discussions and gather data.	• Brainstorming • Interview • Multivoting • Pareto Diagram
5. Identify potential subprocess problems to pursue.	• Evaluate data to identify the potential internal subprocess problems affecting customer satisfaction and costs. • Add each to the list of potential process problems developed during Activity 2. This list will provide the primary candidates for quality improvement projects.	• Nominal Group Technique • Pareto Diagram

Checklist 1   As noted in Activity 1, to investigate opportunities for process simplification, ask questions such as:

- Is the activity needed, that is, does it add value?
- Is the activity performed to accommodate errors, for example, rework?
- Is the activity performed to undo the work of someone else?
- What additional opportunities for creating errors are introduced by rework?
- What are the obvious redundancies?
- Should someone else perform the work activity?
- Should it be combined with other activities?
- Should activities be run in parallel instead of series?

Checklist 2   As noted in Activity 1, to investigate interactions at interfaces, ask questions such as:

- How do things get lost, changed, or misinterpreted between activities?
- Is there adequate communication/feedback between activities?
- Are clear internal customer/supplier requirements established and documented?
- Are roles and responsibilities clearly defined?
- Are there undue delays?
- What practice determines the order in which work is processed, including special cases such as workarounds or ad-hoc procedures?
- Is there a more efficient or effective means of transmitting information or materials?

Example

To understand why the Document Production Center is not meeting the customer requirement of delivering final documents to management within three days, the process management team investigates the process to identify the source of delay.

Gather data on problems

Discussing the diagram produced in **Step 2** (shown below), the process management team interviews people working in the process who identify two major contributors to increased production time:

- Rework in Text Processing
- Rework in Reproduction.

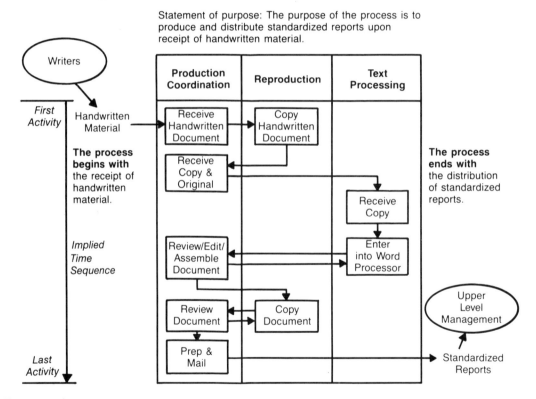

To gauge how much time is lost in rework, the process management team begins tracking the percent of jobs that are returned to Text Processing and Reproduction for rework and the resulting delays.

*Identify
potential
problems
to pursue*

They observe that:

- Rework is required for 8 percent of the jobs produced by Text Processing. On average, this delays document delivery time by one-half day.

- Rework is required for 20 percent of the jobs produced by Reproduction. On average, this delays document delivery time by one day.

The process management team decides to focus its initial problem identification efforts on Reproduction's *copy document* process.

*Document
potential
problem
areas*

To see what may be causing reproduction rework in the copy document process, the process management team produces the following flow diagram and written description.

Flow Diagram

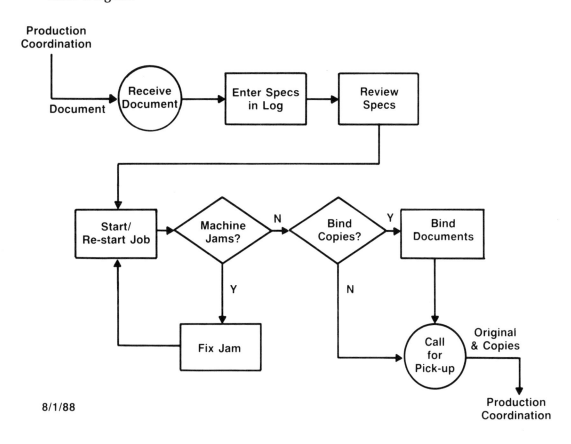

8/1/88

Written Description

> Upon receipt of the document, the on-duty Reproduction Supervisor records all job information in a log. This information includes the number of copies required, whether the job will be one- or two-sided, the weight of the paper stock to be used, and what type of binding is required, if any.
>
> If the job cannot be copied immediately, the Reproduction Supervisor puts it in a waiting line and, generally, it will be handled on a first come, first serve basis. Difficult jobs that must be hand-fed are occasionally preempted by easier batch jobs. Before copying the job, the reproduction machine operator first reviews the job specifications recorded in the log. If the operator has any questions, he or she contacts the supervisor who entered the specifications. If the supervisor is not available, the operator either holds the job or enters his or her own job specifications into the log and runs the job accordingly.
>
> If the document is to be bound, the operator puts it into a second waiting line. From here, it is handled on a first come, first serve basis.

Gather data on subprocess problems

The process management team gathers data on the causes of reproduction rework over a period of several weeks.

Identify potential subprocess problems

The process management team analyzes the data and discovers, as shown in the Pareto diagram below, that approximately 90 percent of the errors leading to reproduction re-work are due to either missing pages, pages out of order, or pages upside down.

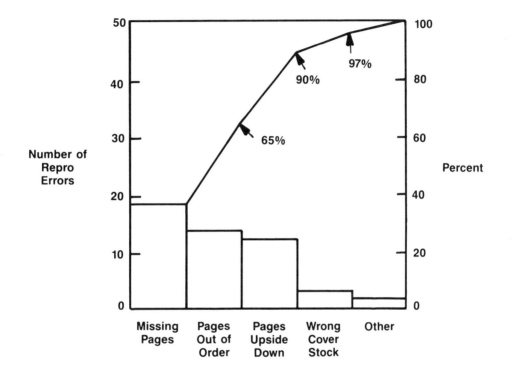

Further analysis, using a cause and effect diagram, leads the process management team to identify *machine jams* as the dominant subprocess problem resulting in missing pages, pages out of order, or pages upside down.

STEP 6: RANK IMPROVEMENT OPPORTUNITIES AND SET OBJECTIVES

"No wise fish would go anywhere without a porpoise... Why, if a fish came to me, and told me he was going on a journey, I should say 'With what porpoise?'"

The Mock Turtle

Overview

Successful process quality improvement depends on determining which process improvement opportunities will best serve *your purpose*, will have the most positive impact on customer satisfaction and meet internal business objectives. To select opportunities wisely and fully realize the benefit of these improvements the process management team must:

- Establish reasonable expectations for the process based on customer needs and process capability

- Make a documented commitment to customers stating the scope and time frame for improvement.

Objectives of this section

This section provides guidelines for:

- Relating improvement objectives to customer requirements and business needs

- Securing buy-in and commitment to improvement objectives

- Rank ordering improvement opportunities and identifying improvement projects.

Ranking opportunities

To rank opportunities and set objectives, perform the activities and tasks in the following table.

Activity	Tasks	Tools
1. Review improvement opportunities.	• Review results of process assessment and investigation. • List improvement opportunities.	
2. Establish priority of each improvement opportunity.	• Rank improvement opportunities based on: — customer needs — internal business objectives — benefit/cost ratio — potential for improvement — resources required to implement improvement — available resources — feasibility.	• Decision Matrix • Graph • Histogram • Multivoting • Nominal Group Technique • Pareto Diagram
3. Negotiate objectives.	• For each high-priority opportunity: — negotiate objectives and timeframes with process improvement participants and suppliers — negotiate overall objectives including time frame for closing the gap between current performance and customer requirements — document commitment to customers.	• Nominal Group Technique
4. Decide on improvement projects.	• Select improvement projects based on priorities established in Activity 2 and objectives negotiated in Activity 3.	

Example

The process management team has begun to address process problems impacting their customers' requirement for document timeliness. At this point, the team needs to determine which specific improvement projects to pursue.

*Review
improvement
opportunities*

In **Step 5**, the process management team identified two areas for improvement that affect document production time:

- Rework by Reproduction

- Rework by Text Processing.

*Establish
priorities*

As indicated in **Step 5**, excessive rework in Reproduction is a major factor affecting end-to-end turnaround time. Reducing this rework has the potential to shorten the turnaround time by one day. The process management team determines that, while opportunity for improvement exists in Text Processing, the most significant improvement in turnaround time will result from focusing efforts on Reproduction, specifically the machine jam problem.

*Negotiate
objectives*

The process management team agrees on the following improvement targets:

- With customers, the center will reduce the delivery interval from an average of 3.7 days to 3 days or less within six months.

- Within the process, the center will reduce the percentage of documents requiring rework by Reproduction from 20 percent to 0 percent within six months.

*Decide on
improvement
projects*

The process management team decides to focus immediate process quality improvement efforts on reproduction errors resulting in rework and, more specifically, on machine jams.

STEP 7: IMPROVE PROCESS QUALITY

"there's half my plan done...I've got to my right size: the next thing is, to get into that beautiful garden—how is that to be done, I wonder?"

Alice

Overview

At the beginning of her adventures, Alice glimpsed the bright flowers and cool fountains and knew where she wanted to go. But only when she had become the right size could she find her way into the beautiful garden.

A similar tantalizing glimpse—a vision of the benefits of a more effective and efficient process— has motivated your journey through the first six steps of these guidelines. "Half your plan is done" when you have successfully completed these six steps: You thoroughly understand your process—how it works, how well it works, and where it should work better. Now you can logically focus on sustained process *improvement*.

Step 7 provides a structured approach to carrying out the second part of your plan, to achieve continuous process quality improvement. In general, the approach requires the development of an action plan and diagnosis of root causes of process problems— with solutions tested, evaluated, and refined—before implementation of any solutions. This avoids the practice of treating the symptoms, rather than the true causes of problems. Once process improvement is realized, follow-through is essential to ensure that the results of your improvement efforts do not deteriorate over time.

Objectives of this section

This section provides guidelines for:
- Organizing quality improvement teams
- Applying the root cause approach to process quality improvement rather than the quick fix (band-aid) approach
- Applying specific techniques for identifying and removing root causes of problems
- Sustaining a new process performance level.

Alternate routes

Your process management team (PMT) may actually perform the quality improvement activities, serving, in effect, as the quality improvement team. Alternatively, you may assign these activities to individual quality improvement teams (QIT) when, for example, you have identified several quality improvement projects. These quality improvement teams are typically established to work on "single event" improvement areas; they usually disband when the improvements are achieved. In both cases, the process management team is responsible for organizing, supporting, and tracking the quality improvement effort and for follow-through and evaluation to ensure that new levels of process performance are sustained.

This section includes two versions of **Step 7**, describing specific activities and tasks for

- the process management team functioning as the quality improvement team (**PMT as QIT**) to perform the quality improvement cycle activities [1]
- the process management team working with quality improvement teams (**PMT plus QITs**) to complete quality improvement efforts.

Quality improvement roadmap

This figure illustrates the alternate routes to sustained process quality improvement, as described above.

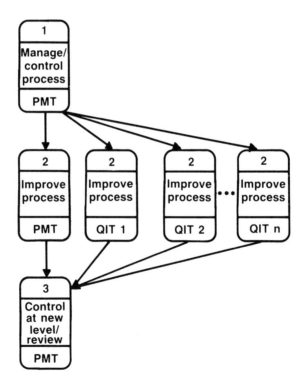

| Quality improvement team | Forming the quality improvement team is an important step in process improvement. Whether the process management team serves as the quality improvement team or recruits quality improvement team members from the process at large, it is important that some members of the quality improvement team satisfy each of the following criteria: |

- Detailed understanding of the process and of the improvement project's link to the process
- High-level view of the process and appreciation of the impact of process changes on end-to-end performance*
- Skill in the techniques of process quality improvement
- Experience with the problem (affected by the problem) or ability solve the problem.

Note that because a problem may have its root cause in another functional organization members of the quality improvement team may be drawn from several functional organizations.

| Improving your process: PMT as QIT | To improve your process, perform the activities and tasks in the following table. If the PMT chooses to delegate quality improvement projects, refer to **Improving your process: PMT plus QITs** (page 59) for process management team responsibilities and activities and a summary of recommended quality improvement team activities. |

Activity	Tasks	Tools
1. Organize team; develop action plan.[4]	• Organize quality improvement team: — Include representatives from major areas involved in the process. — Identify roles and responsibilities: Team Leader (coordinate activities, provide resources, motivate members) Facilitator (facilitates meetings) Team Member (identify improvement opportunities, gather data, analyze causes). • Clarify problem statement and objectives. • Establish schedule/budget. • Review plan with process owner and implementors.	• Action Plan • Problem Definition Checklist

---

* Often, a member of the process management team will fill this role, providing a direct link between the improvement project and overall process objectives.

Activity	Tasks	Tools
2. Determine root causes[5] (diagnostic journey).	• Perform cause and effect analysis on the problem to the level of root cause. • Select actionable root causes. • Support potential root causes with data. • Select vital root causes, those having the greatest probable impact.	• Cause and Effect Diagram • Data Collection Form • Graph • Histogram • Pareto Diagram
3. Test and implement solution[5] (remedial journey).	For each vital root cause: • Develop and select potential solutions. • Test, evaluate, and revise solutions. • Implement and monitor solutions.	• Action Plan • Cause and Effect/ Force Field Analysis • Decision Matrix
4. Hold the gains (follow through).	• Develop required education and training. • Publish revised methods and procedures. • Establish tracking system to monitor results. • Determine areas for replication. • Plan further actions, if necessary. • Evaluate implementation of improvement cycle. • Repeat **Step 4, Assess Conformance to Customer Requirements** — Monitor performance — Collect and communicate customer feedback on performance. • Repeat **Step 2, Define Process and Identify Customer Requirements** — Review requirements and establish new requirements, as appropriate.	• Action Plan • Control Chart • Graph • Histogram
5. Perform periodic process review.	• Invite outside experts to review application of the PQMI methodology. • Document/publish results. • Take corrective actions, as required.	

Improving your process: PMT plus QITs

When the process management team appoints quality improvement teams:

- the process management team fills a support and oversight role to ensure "process fit" of planned improvement, including monitoring
- the quality improvement team implements the quality improvement cycle.

This table lists process management team activities and tasks in support of quality improvement projects delegated to quality improvement teams.

Process management team activities

Activity	Tasks	Tools
1. Organize quality improvement teams.	• Decide on a team leader, a facilitator, and team members. • Include — Representatives from major areas involved in the process — Member of process management team. • Identify roles and responsibilities: — Team Leader (coordinate activities, provide resources, motivate members link to PMT) — Facilitator (facilitates meetings) — Team Member (identify improvement opportunities, gather data, analyze causes).	
2. Provide resources, direction.	• Develop schedule, budget. • Support with training, quality improvement cycle methodology.	
3. Monitor and review.	• Review quality improvement action plans. • Review root causes and proposed solutions. • Review test/implementation results.	• Data Collection Form

Activity	Tasks	Tools
4. Hold the gains (follow through).	• Control at new level. • Establish and communicate revised procedures. • Standardize to ensure uniform application. • Train in new procedures. • Review with quality improvement team the strengths and weaknesses of the improvement project. • Repeat **Step 4, Assess Conformance to Customer Requirements** — Monitor performance — Collect and communicate customer feedback on performance. • Repeat **Step 2, Define Process and Identify Customer Requirements** — Review requirements and establish new requirements, as appropriate.	• Action Plan • Control Chart • Graph • Histogram
5. Perform periodic process review.	• Invite outside experts to review application of the PQMI methodology. • Document/publish results. • Take corrective actions, as required.	

Quality improvement team activities

Quality improvement teams should follow the quality improvement cycle described in the *AT&T Quality Improvement Cycle*,[1] working with the process management team to realize sustained process improvement. This table summarizes the steps in the quality improvement methodology. In some cases the process management team may have already developed detailed process analysis information. This information may enable the quality improvement team to move directly from planning (Activity 1) to focusing on improvement opportunities (Activity 5).

Quality
Improvement
Cycle

Activity	Tasks
1. Select improvement area.	• Clarify problem statement and objectives. • Develop schedule/budget. • Review plan with process owner, implementer, and/or management.
2. Identify outputs and customers.	• Identify outputs. • Identify customers.
3. Determine customer expectations.	• Identify characteristics, customer requirements, and priorities. • Establish measures and collect data. • Assess conformance to requirements, describe gap.
4. Describe current process.	• Identify inputs, suppliers. • Flowchart the process. • Collect data. • Assess process performance, establish targets.
5. Focus on improvement opportunities.	• Select opportunities to pursue.
6. Determine root causes (diagnostic journey).	• Perform cause and effect analysis on the problem to the level of root cause. • Select actionable root causes. • Support potential root causes with data. • Select vital root causes (greatest probable impact). • Review findings with PMT.
7. Trial and implement solution (remedial journey).	• Develop and select potential solutions. • Develop an action plan. • Test, evaluate, and revise solutions. • Implement and monitor solutions.
8. Hold the gains (follow through).	• Recommend to PMT — required education and revised methods and procedures — areas for replication. • Plan further actions, if necessary. • Evaluate implementation of improvement cycle.

Process review

A process review is an objective assessment that reveals how well you have applied the methodology to your process. The review emphasizes the potential for long-term process results rather than the actual results achieved. The following table is a guide to help you assess your process.[6] It includes assessment criteria and suggestions for interpreting the results of the review.

Assessment Criteria	Potential for Long-Term Results
Basic elements of process quality management not in place.	Low effectiveness and low efficiency.
Basic elements in place. • Process owner assigned and responsibilities defined. • Process defined and needs analysis conducted. • Adequate quality measures defined and control system established for process inputs and outputs. • Procedures documented. • System for ongoing data collection and periodic reporting implemented. • Ongoing education and training in job-related and quality techniques. • Satisfaction feedback system established for customers. • Customer requirements reviewed periodically. • Process reviews conducted periodically.	Effective and efficient process.
Basic elements in place and being applied in a disciplined manner.	Highly effective and highly efficient process.

Example

To further reduce reproduction errors resulting in excessive rework, the Document Production Center initiates the following activities. Note that because the process management team has thoroughly investigated the process, and because of considerable overlap in the membership of the quality improvement team and the process management team, the quality improvement team is able to move directly from planning to a focus on improvement opportunities.

Develop action plan

A quality improvement team is formed, consisting of the Reproduction Supervisor as the team leader, two reproduction operators, the Production Coordinator, and a facilitator. At the first meeting, the quality improvement team reviews and clarifies the problem with reproduction errors, developing a clear problem statement in customer terms and in terms of a measurable gap in performance. The team agrees to meet with members of the Reproduction group to analyze possible causes. They present their plan to the Center Manager, who requests the cooperation of personnel in the affected areas.

Determine root causes

In **Step 5**, the process management team determined that rework resulting from missing pages, pages out of order, and pages upside down, etc. is a symptom of machine jams. Using a cause and effect diagram, the quality improvement team determines that the dominant root cause of machine jams is undetected cut-and-paste pages fed through the machine.

Trial and implement solution

The quality improvement team discusses several alternative methods of handling the cut-and-paste pages before agreeing on a final solution. The team decides on a new method whereby cut-and-paste pages, submitted to Reproduction by Production Coordination, are secured on all sides with transparent tape and all such pages are clearly marked. This simple internal requirement between Production Coordination and Reproduction virtually eliminates the machine jam problem, significantly reducing reproduction rework and making the 3-day delivery interval a reality.

Hold the gain

Following through on this improvement, the internal requirement for special handling of cut-and-paste pages is made part of standard procedure. This requirement is documented and distributed to all the members of Production Coordination, Reproduction, and Text Processing. Performance in terms of closing the gap is continually monitored to ensure lasting results. Also, all customers are surveyed every three months, and feedback is shared with center members.

Perform periodic process reviews

After new process standards are in effect for about one year, the Center Manager requests a review of process operations to:

- Determine the extent to which new methods and practices are being effectively applied

- Assess whether disciplined application of quality management and improvement steps is continuing

- Identify further opportunities for improvement.

The review is conducted by experts in process quality evaluation.

SUMMARY CHART

"'You must remember,' remarked the King... "

Overview This section provides a quick reference chart to help you remember the key information in **Part Two**. The chart lists the objective of each step in the methodology, the activities that you perform to meet the objective, and the supporting tools available to you.

SUMMARY OF STEPS

STEPS	OBJECTIVES	KEY ACTIVITIES	TOOLS/ TECHNIQUES
1. Establish process management responsibilities. **Owner**	• Identify the owner in charge of the end-to-end process. • Identify responsibility of all process members.	• Review owner selection criteria. • Identify owner and process members. • Establish review responsibilities of owner and process members.	• Multivoting • Nominal Group Technique
2. Define process and identify customer requirements.	• Understand how the process operates at a high level and what is required of it.	• Define process boundaries and major groups, outputs and customers, inputs and suppliers, and subprocesses and flows. • Conduct customer needs analysis. • Define customer requirements and communicate your own requirements to suppliers.	• Affinity Diagram • Benchmarking • Block Diagram • Customer Needs Analysis • Customer/Supplier Questionnaire • Interview • Q-MAP • Survey • Tree Diagram
3. Define and establish measures. **Measurements** M1 M2 M3	• Determine what needs to be measured and controlled to meet customer requirements.	• Decide on effective measures. • Review existing measures. • Install new measures and reporting system. • Establish customer satisfaction feedback system.	• Brainstorming • Interview • Multivoting • Nominal Group Technique • Q-MAP • Survey
4. Assess conformance to customer requirements.	• Find out how well you are doing against customer requirements and how well suppliers are doing against your requirements.	• Collect and review data on process operations. • Identify and remove causes of abnormal variation. • Compare performance of stable process to requirements and determine chronic problem areas.	• Brainstorming • Cause and Effect Diagram • Control Chart • Graph • Interview • Multivoting • Nominal Group Technique • Pareto Diagram • Q-MAP • Survey

SUMMARY OF STEPS (Cont'd)

STEPS	OBJECTIVES	KEY ACTIVITIES	TOOLS/ TECHNIQUES
5. Investigate process to identify improvement opportunities.	• Identify internal process problems affecting customer satisfaction and costs. • Identify process simplification opportunities.	• Gather data on process problems. • Identify potential process problem areas to pursue. • Document potential problem areas. • Gather data on subprocess problems. • Identify potential subprocess problems to pursue.	• Brainstorming • Flowchart • Interview • Multivoting • Nominal Group Technique • Pareto Diagram
6. Rank improvement opportunities and set objectives.	• Decide on order of fixing problems. • Set targets for improvement.	• Review improvement opportunities. • Establish priorities. • Negotiate objectives. • Decide on improvement projects.	• Decision Matrix • Graph • Histogram • Multivoting • Nominal Group Technique • Pareto Diagram
7. Improve process quality (apply Quality Improvement Cycle).	• Achieve new level of process performance.	• Organize team and develop action plan. • Determine root causes (diagnostic journey) • Test and implement solution (remedial journey). • Hold the gains • Perform periodic process review.	• Action Plan • Cause and Effect Diagram • Cause and Effect/Force Field Analysis • Control Chart • Data Collection Form • Decision Matrix • Flowchart • Graph • Histogram • Pareto Diagram • Problem Definition Checklist

A • P • P • E • N • D • I • X

TOOLS & TECHNIQUES

"The chief difficulty Alice found at first was in managing the flamingo...and when she got its head down...it was very provoking to find that the hedgehog had unrolled himself and was in the act of crawling away."

The Croquet Game

Alice knew that she could play better croquet with a mallet and a ball. Success in any endeavor depends not only on having the right strategy, but also on having the tools to support that strategy. This appendix describes the tools and techniques that will help you to perform successfully the activities and tasks recommended throughout these guidelines, thereby implementing effective quality management and improvement programs.

TOOLS & TECHNIQUES

Overview   This appendix describes the tools and techniques recommended to support process quality management and improvement activities. The appendix is arranged in alphabetical order for ease of access. Although not exhaustive, it includes many of the most useful tools and techniques.

Process Management Tools

- Affinity Diagram/ KJ Method
- Benchmarking
- Block Diagram
- Brainstorming
- Cause and Effect Diagram
- Cause and Effect/Force Field Analysis
- Control Chart
- Customer-Needs Analysis
- Customer/Supplier Questionnaire

- Flowchart
- Graph
- Interview
- Multivoting
- Nominal Group Technique
- Pareto Diagram
- Q-MAP
- Survey
- Tree Diagram

Process Improvement Tools

- Action Plan
- Block Diagram
- Brainstorming
- Cause and Effect Diagram
- Cause and Effect/Force Field Analysis
- Control Chart
- Customer-Needs Analysis
- Customer/Supplier Model
- Customer/Supplier Questionnaire
- Data Collection Form

- Decision Matrix
- Flowchart
- Graph
- Histogram
- Interview
- Multivoting
- Nominal Group Technique
- Pareto Diagram
- Problem Definition Checklist
- Survey

When to use	Use...	When you need to...
	Action Plan	Explain implementation plans to management and workers, and ensure an organized, objective implementation.
	Affinity Diagram/ KJ Method	Organize into groupings a large number of ideas, opinions, issues, or other concerns.
	Benchmarking	Measure your process against those of recognized leaders.
	Block Diagram	Obtain a macro-level view of the process as it currently operates.
	Brainstorming	Generate, clarify, and evaluate a sizable list of ideas, problems, or issues.
	Cause and Effect Diagram	Systematically analyze cause and effect relationships and identify potential root causes of a problem.
	Cause and Effect/Force Field Analysis	Identify problems, their causes, and the driving and restraining forces that affect process performance.
	Control Chart	Monitor the performance of a process with frequent outputs to determine if its performance reveals normal variations or out-of-control conditions.
	Customer-Needs Analysis	Identify what customers expect of us, their requirements, and what we have jointly agreed to provide.
	Customer/Supplier Model	Understand your process from a customer perspective.
	Customer/Supplier Questionnaire	Assess your relationship with your customers and suppliers, and start focusing on your process performance.
	Data Collection Form	Gather a variety of data in a systematic fashion for a clear and objective picture of the facts.

Use...	When you need to...
Decision Matrix	Select from a group of potential problems or solutions those having the greatest impact, need for attention, etc.
Flowchart	Describe an existing process, develop modifications, or design an entirely new process.
Graphs: Bar, Line, Pie	Visually display complex and quantifiable data.
Histogram	Display the dispersion or spread of data.
Interview	Broaden the team's foundation of knowledge and identify people not on the team who are sources of needed information.
Multivoting	Accomplish "list reduction" and assignment of priorities quickly and with a high degree of group agreement.
Nominal Group Technique	Reach consensus within a structured situation.
Pareto Diagram	Identify major factors and distinguish between the "vital few" causes and the potentially less significant ones.
Problem Definition Checklist	State specifically the improvement opportunity the team is addressing.
Q-MAP	Select and develop customized measures of process performance by means of a personal computer software tool.
Survey	Determine customer needs for a large group of customers.
Tree Diagram	Define a hierarchy of needs, objectives, characteristics, or goals.

Action Plan

Application   Step 7: Improve Process Quality

Description   The Action Plan[9] is a catalog of the activities required to ensure a smooth and objective trial and implementation of a solution. Although its format may vary, the Action Plan should identify who, what, when, where, and how and should document obstacles and advantages of the plan.

Procedure
1. Break the proposed solution implementation into steps.
2. Identify the materials and numbers of people involved at each step.
3. Brainstorm, if necessary, for other items of possible significance.
4. Add to the list until you think it is complete.

Illustration

Action Plan

Prepared by _____ Date _____ Page __ of __

TASK ASSIGNMENT RECORD   Loc./Proj. _____ Period _____

No.	Task/ Project	Priority Due Date	Assigned To	Date Assigned	Status/ Remarks

Affinity Diagram/KJ Method

Application   Step 2: Define Process and Identify Customer Requirements

Description   When large numbers of ideas, opinions, issues, and other concerns are being collected, this tool[7] organizes the information into groupings based on the natural relationships that exist among them. The process is designed to stimulate creativity and full participation. It works best in groups of limited size (maximum of eight members recommended), in which members are accustomed to working together. This tool is often used to organize ideas generated by brainstorming.

Procedure

1. State the issue in broad terms (details may prejudice the responses).

2. Record individual responses on small cards.

3. Mix the cards and spread them randomly on a large table.

4. Group related cards together:

   - Sort cards that seem to be related into groups.

   - Limit number of groupings to ten without force-fitting single cards into groups.

   - Locate or create a header card that captures the meaning of the group.

   - Place this header card on top.

5. Transfer the information from cards onto paper, outlined by groupings.

Illustration   This figure shows an Affinity Diagram for a telephone answering machine.

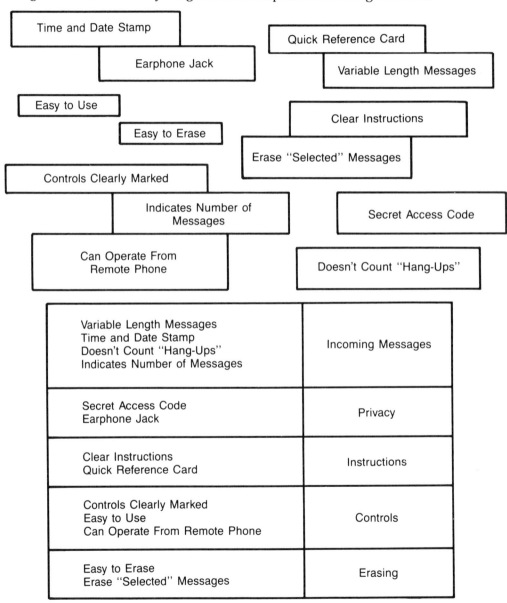

Benchmarking

Application	Step 2: Define Process and Identify Customer Requirements

Description Benchmarking[8] measures your processes against those of recognized leaders. It helps you to establish priorities and targets that will lead to competitive advantage in the marketplace.

Procedure

1. Determine what items to benchmark. The items should be key characteristics of your process output directly related to your customers' needs.

2. Determine who to benchmark: companies, organizations, or groups who are direct competitors and/or noncompetitors with a "best in class" reputation and key similarities such as:
   - Type of process, for example, billing and shipping
   - Characteristics/nature of work, for example, type of customers, size, outputs.

3. Determine benchmarks:
   - Collect data by means of direct contact, surveys, interviews, personal and professional contacts, technical journals, advertisements, etc.
   - Analyze data.

4. For each benchmark item identified above, determine the "best in class" target for direct competitors and noncompetitors.

Requirements are based on both customer needs and benchmarking targets.

- If the results of benchmarking determine that direct competitor's performance exceeds your customers' needs, then your requirements must be at least as good as the best direct competitor targets.
- If the results of benchmarking determine that no direct competitors achieve your customers' needs, and if
  — noncompetitors also do not achieve customer needs, then you should reevaluate customer needs.
  — noncompetitors achieve customer needs, then your requirements should be as good as your customers' needs.

Block Diagram

Application Step 2: Define Process and Identify Customer Requirements

Description The block diagram helps to develop a common understanding at a high level of how the process is currently operating and how major work groups within the process interact and interface with outside organizations. The diagram traces the various paths that materials and information can take between input from suppliers and final outputs. The diagram includes individual boxes or *blocks* representing activities performed by individual organizations/groups and connecting lines representing the hand-off points or interfaces between activities.

Procedure

1. Define the purpose and boundaries of the process.

2. Draw a box containing columns for

   - each of the major work groups within your process

   - customers and suppliers external to the process.

   Label the top of each column with the group name.

3. For each input to your process identify the supplier and define the work activity that it feeds. Draw and label a representative activity box in the appropriate column.

4. For each activity defined, determine the output it produces, the activity or customer who receives the output, and the individual or group who performs the activity. Document this information on the diagram.

5. Label each new activity box and continue generating work/information flows and work activities until you connect into all process outputs defined to the right of the process box.

6. Verify with members of major work groups that the diagram accurately reflects the way the process currently works.

Illustration   This figure shows a block diagram for the document production process.

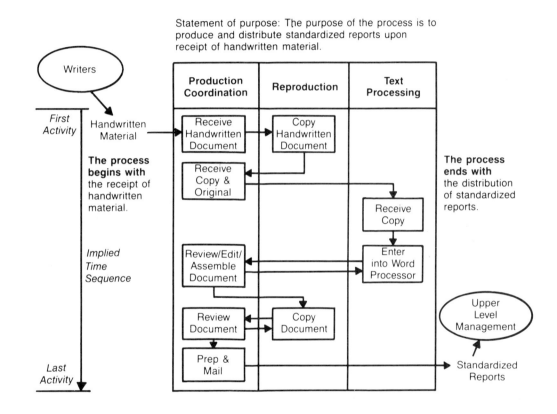

Statement of purpose: The purpose of the process is to produce and distribute standardized reports upon receipt of handwritten material.

Brainstorming

Application	Step 3: Define and Establish Measures
	Step 4: Assess Conformance to Customer Requirements
	Step 5: Investigate Process to Identify Improvement Opportunities

Description Brainstorming[9] is an excellent technique for tapping the creative thinking of a team to quickly generate, clarify, and evaluate a sizable list of ideas, problems, issues, etc.

- In the **Generation Phase**, the team leader reviews the rules for brainstorming and the team members generate a list of items. The objective is *quantity*, not quality of ideas.

- In the **Clarification Phase**, the team goes over the list to make sure that everyone understands all the items. Discussion will take place later.

- Finally, in the **Evaluation Phase**, the team reviews the list to eliminate duplications, irrelevancies, or issues that are off limits.

Rules for Brainstorming

- State the purpose clearly.
- Each person may take a turn in sequence, or ideas may be expressed spontaneously.
- Offer one thought at a time.
- Don't criticize ideas.
- Don't discuss ideas.
- Build on others' ideas.
- Record all ideas where they are visible to team members.

Note: Brainstorming is a subjective technique that must later be substantiated by data.

Cause and Effect (Fishbone) Diagram

Application   Step 4: Assess Conformance to Customer Requirements

Step 7: Improve Process Quality

Description   A Cause and Effect[10,11] or Fishbone Diagram represents the relationships between a given effect and its potential causes (cause and effect analysis). Cause and Effect Diagrams are drawn to sort out and relate the interactions among the factors affecting a process. A well-detailed Cause and Effect Diagram will take the shape of a fishbone, hence its alias.

Procedure

1. Define the problem (effect) clearly and objectively.

2. Define the major categories of possible causes. Use generic branches.

    Factors to consider include:

    - Data and Information Systems
    - Dollars
    - Environment
    - Hardware
    - Materials

    - Measurements
    - Methods
    - People
    - Training

3. Begin to construct the diagram, defining the effect in a box at left and positioning major categories as "feeders" to the effect box.

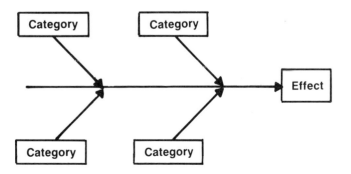

4. Brainstorm possible causes within major categories and position these to feed into related categories.

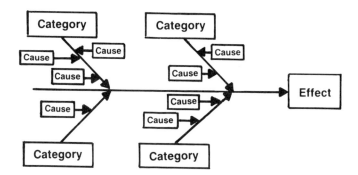

5. Analyze each cause to focus in on more and more specific causes.

6. Identify and circle the likely and actionable root causes.

7. Gather data to verify the most likely root cause(s). A Pareto diagram is a good way to display this data.

Example

This figure shows a Cause and Effect Diagram for poor photocopy quality.

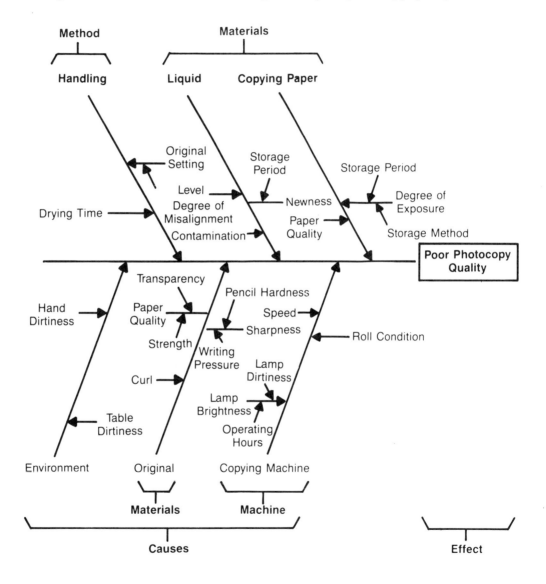

Cause and Effect/Force Field Analysis

Application   Step 7: Improve Process Quality

Description   Cause and Effect/Force Field Analysis (CEFFA)[12] is a combination of Cause and Effect Analysis and Force Field Analysis. CEFFA is used to identify problems, their causes, and the driving and restraining forces that affect process performance.

Procedure

1. Select the problem.

    A group of six to ten people and an individual trained in CEFFA techniques brainstorm the quality problems (*effects*) and then reach consensus on one effect that is the most significant.

2. Construct Cause and Effect (fishbone) Diagram.

    Led by a facilitator, the group constructs a diagram that documents potential causes related to the effect.

3. Rank order these causes according to their level of importance.

    This figure shows a rank-ordered list of causes related to failure to achieve effective implementation of a quality training and education proposal.

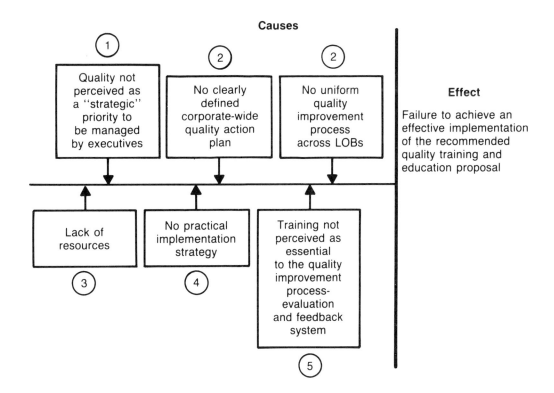

4. Perform Force Field Analysis.

   The group identifies the *restraining forces* that are keeping the problem at its current level (the causes of the problem) and the *driving forces* that are pushing the problem toward improvement (the solutions to the problem).

   In this figure the most important cause is identified as, "the level of perception of quality." Restraining forces push the problem *down* toward its current level, represented by the horizontal line.

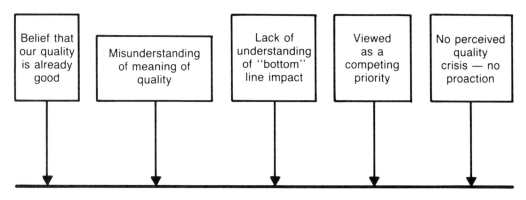

Level of Perception of Quality as a Strategic Priority is too LOW

Belief that our quality is already good	Misunderstanding of meaning of quality	Lack of understanding of ''bottom'' line impact	Viewed as a competing priority	No perceived quality crisis — no proaction

Restraining Forces

After identifying the relevant restraining forces, the group looks for driving forces to counter the restraining forces. In the following figure, the upward arrows are pointing the driving forces toward their associated restraining forces. To clarify the results, the driving forces are numbered and the restraining forces are lettered. The key lists the three driving forces and the associated restraining forces.

**Level of Perception of Quality as a Strategic
Priority is too LOW**

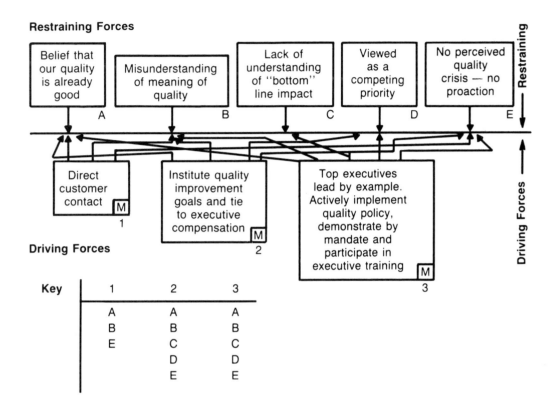

Restraining Forces

| Belief that our quality is already good | Misunderstanding of meaning of quality | Lack of understanding of "bottom" line impact | Viewed as a competing priority | No perceived quality crisis — no proaction |

A   B   C   D   E

Restraining

| Direct customer contact [M] | Institute quality improvement goals and tie to executive compensation [M] | Top executives lead by example. Actively implement quality policy, demonstrate by mandate and participate in executive training [M] |

1   2   3

Driving Forces

Driving Forces

Key	1	2	3
	A	A	A
	B	B	B
	E	C	C
		D	D
		E	E

5. Summarize the diagram.

    The completed force field analysis diagram provides a list of possible solutions to the identified quality problem. Next, the group determines ownership of the problem and identifies management (**M**) or worker (**W**) alongside the respective driving force. If possible, the responsible individual should be identified by name. Since, in this example, the problem deals with a high-level strategic business issue, management owns 100 percent of the driving forces.

    To complete the analysis, the results are documented and presented to the appropriate level of management for action.

Control Charts

Application   Step 4: Assess Conformance to Customer Requirements

Step 7: Improve Process Quality

Description   Control charts[9,13,14] monitor the ongoing performance of a process. They show departures from a standard, objective, or average and illustrate the level of statistical control of a process over time. They can be used to study process capability, to help define achievable quality objectives, and to detect changes in process average and variability that require corrective action.

Control charts are based on four concepts:

- All processes fluctuate with time.

- Individual points are unpredictable.

- A stable process fluctuates randomly, and groups of points from a stable process tend to fall within predictable bounds.

- An unstable process does not fluctuate randomly, and the nonrandom fluctuations are generally those that fall outside of predictable boundaries.

Control charts allow you to use current operating data to establish statistically normal operating limits (control limits). They can be used to determine whether fluctuation is normal (in control) or abnormal (out of control). Normal operating limits consist of the average value plus or minus three standard deviations. This gives you a "range" of normal operations that will result in some of your points appearing above the center (average) line and some below, but 99.75 percent within the boundaries of the Upper Control Limit (UCL) and the Lower Control Limit (LCL).

**Using
control
charts**

To use the control chart, you examine the location of the data points. If your process is basically consistent and stable, most of the data points fall within the established limits. Points that fall outside one of the control limits can be reported or investigated.

Continued use of the control chart can help to determine whether or not your operations are *staying* within established operating limits.

To obtain useful information about process performance, you must also establish customer requirements for process output and acceptable variation (which may be zero). This constitutes process requirements. Actual output of the process is measured over time and compared with these process requirements to determine that the process is

- Out of control but capable of meeting customer requirements (process control/management required).

- In control but incapable of meeting customer requirements (process improvement required).

- Out of control and incapable of meeting customer requirements (process control/management required; process improvement required).

Choosing the right chart

The type of Control Chart you use depends on the type of data you collect. This figure can help you to determine what type of control chart to use.

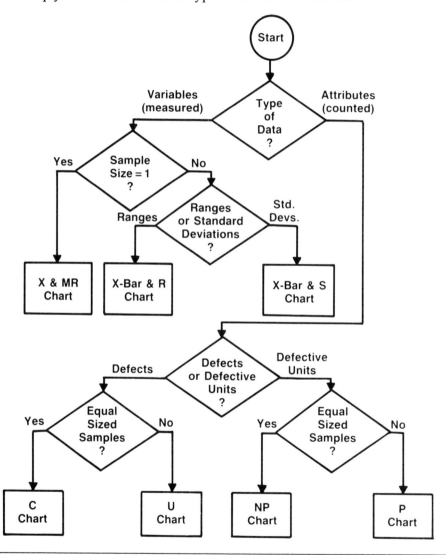

Procedure

1. Select the control chart type(s) appropriate to your data and process characteristics.

2. Decide what you want to measure, and record measurement data on the vertical axis.

3. Divide the data into subgroups or measurement intervals according to date, time, lot, etc. Plot the subgroups on the horizontal axis.

4. Calculate the average value and control limits.

5. Mark these points on the vertical axis, and draw horizontal lines from their respective values.

6. Complete the chart by plotting the observations.

Refer to the *AT&T Statistical Quality Control Handbook*[14] for detailed instructions on creating and interpreting control charts.

Illustration

This figure shows X-bar and R control charts used to track delivery time over a 10-week period. The two charts show a process that is in a state of statistical control because performance is fluctuating within the upper and lower control limits. However, if you compare the long-term delivery interval (average of 3.7 days on X-bar chart) to the customer requirement of three days, you can see that, although the process is in control, it is not capable of meeting customer requirements consistently. The process needs to be improved.

Sample charts

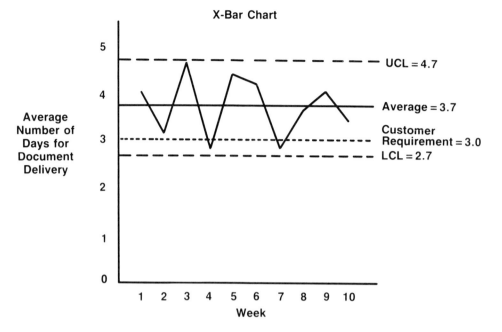

X-Bar Chart

Average Number of Days for Document Delivery

UCL = 4.7

Average = 3.7

Customer Requirement = 3.0

LCL = 2.7

Week

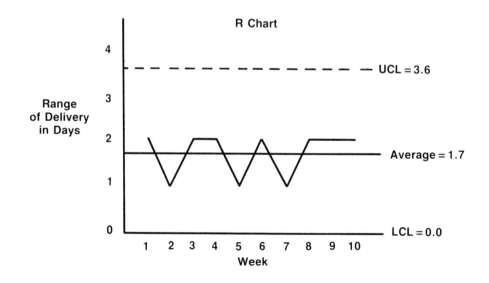

R Chart

Range of Delivery in Days

UCL = 3.6

Average = 1.7

LCL = 0.0

Week

Sample data   The data used to construct the control charts is shown in the following table. Five documents (observations) of the same type were sampled each week over a period of ten weeks (subgroups).

Document Production & Delivery Time

Week (subgroup)	Observations					ΣX	$\overline{X}$	R
	X_1	X_2	X_3	X_4	X_5			
1	4	3	4	4	5	20	4.0	2
2	3	3	3	3	4	16	3.2	1
3	4	4	6	5	4	23	4.6	2
4	3	2	2	3	4	14	2.8	2
5	5	5	4	4	4	22	4.4	1
6	5	3	4	4	5	21	4.2	2
7	2	3	3	3	3	14	2.8	1
8	3	3	3	5	4	18	3.6	2
9	4	4	4	3	5	20	4.0	2
10	4	2	4	4	3	17	3.4	2

Calculations   The calculations are as follows:

Number of observations in each subgroup = 5.
Number of subgroups = 10.

ΣX (for a subgroup) = Sum of observations in a subgroup.

$$\overline{X} \text{ (for a subgroup)} = \frac{\Sigma X \text{ (for a subgroup)}}{\text{Number of observations in that group}} = \text{Sample average (for a subgroup).}$$

$$R \text{ (for a subgroup)} = \text{Largest observation} - \text{Smallest observation}$$
$$\text{(for that subgroup)} \quad \text{(for that subgroup)}$$

$$= \text{Sample range}$$
$$\text{(for a subgroup)}.$$

The average and control limits plotted on the control charts are calculated as follows.

For the R chart:

$$\bar{R} = \text{Average} = \frac{\text{Sum of R values}}{\text{Number of subgroups}} = \frac{17}{10} = 1.7.$$

$$\text{UCL} = \text{Upper Control Limit} = D_4\bar{R} = (2.11)(1.7) = 3.6.$$

$$\text{LCL} = \text{Lower Control Limit} = D_3\bar{R} = (0.0)(1.7) = 0.0.$$

For the X-bar chart:

$$\bar{\bar{X}} = \text{Average} = \frac{\text{Sum of } \bar{X} \text{ values}}{\text{Number of subgroups}} = \frac{37}{10} = 3.7.$$

$$\text{UCL} = \text{Upper Control Limit} = \bar{\bar{X}} + A_2\bar{R} = 3.7 + (0.58)(1.7) = 4.7.$$

$$\text{LCL} = \text{Lower Control Limit} = \bar{\bar{X}} - A_2\bar{R} = 3.7 - (0.58)(1.7) = 2.7.$$

Note: D_4, D_3, A_2 are factors used in calculating control limits for the X-bar and R charts. D_4 and D_3 are used for the R chart upper and lower control limits respectively, A_2 for the X-bar chart control limits. For subgroups of size 5, their values are: $D_2 = 2.11$, $D_3 = 0$, and $A_2 = 0.58$.

Customer-Needs Analysis

Application	Step 2: Define Process and Identify Customer Requirements

Description   Customer-Needs Analysis is the process of determining the key, measurable characteristics that are important to your customer. Customer-Needs Analysis is an effort between the team and the customers to answer these questions:

- What are the **major outputs** of our process?

- Who are the **customers** (both immediate and downstream) for each of these outputs?

- What do our customers say are the **key quality characteristics** that they need in our outputs?

- How can we **measure** our performance on these key characteristics?

- What **goal** would our customers like to see us achieve on these measures?

Key quality characteristics   Possible key quality characteristics are:

Accuracy	Flexibility	Timeliness
Completeness	Relevance	Understandability
Consistency	Reliability	Uniformity

Potential measurements   Potential measurements are:

Cost	Physical parameters
Customer satisfaction	Time
Defects and rework	Work output

Gathering information

Potential methods of determining customer needs are:

- Interviews with
  - Customers
  - Sales personnel
  - Business office personnel

- Mail and telephone market surveys
- Business office complaints analysis
- Executive complaint analysis

Customer/Supplier Model

Applications   Step 2: Define Process and Identify Customer Requirements

Step 4: Assess Conformance to Customer Requirements

Description

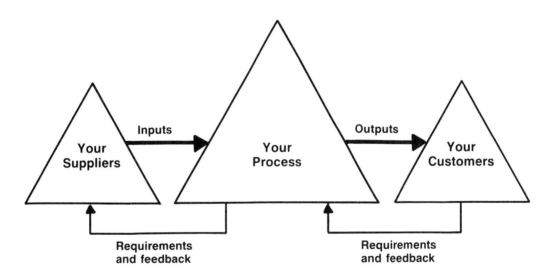

The Customer/Supplier Model is a tool to help focus on the basic elements of your process from a customer perspective:

- **Supplier:** the source of the inputs to your process; may be an individual or group, internal or external to the company

- **Input:** materials and/or information on which your process operates to produce specific outputs

- **Customer**: the individual or group (internal or external to the company) that purchases or receives the product or service output from your process

- **Output**: the product or service your process produces (input + value added)

- **Requirements**: the critical characteristics of process output (based on customer needs and expectations) with associated performance standards

- **Feedback**: communication between customer and supplier about how process output compares with customer expectations

---

Procedure

1. Define the process or task.

2. Define your value-added contribution to the process or task.

3. Define the boundaries of your process. (The process begins with..., ends with...)

4. Define process outputs, customers.

5. Define process inputs, suppliers.

6. Communicate with customers to establish

   - specific requirements based on customer needs and expectations

   - appropriate measurements to determine that process output conforms with requirements

   - regular feedback mechanism (interview, questionnaire, etc.) to ensure the validity and adequacy of requirements and their associated measurements and to ensure that requirements represent full customer satisfaction.

7. Establish *your* requirements and feedback with your supplier(s) just as you did with your customers.

Customer/Supplier Questionnaire

Application	Step 2: Define Process and Identify Customer Requirements

Description
: The questionnaire supports the application of the customer/supplier model. It is used to help you assess your relationship with your customers and suppliers, enabling you to start focusing on your process performance.

Ask questions about your relationship with your customers:

1. What are your primary outputs—information, products, and/or services—as a supplier?
2. Who are your customers—the primary, direct users or recipients of your outputs?
3. What are your customers' requirements for your outputs?
4. How do you determine their requirements?
5. How satisfied are your customers with your outputs?
6. How do you measure their satisfaction?

Ask questions to solicit feedback about your process performance:

1. What output characteristics can be measured to determine whether output meets customers' requirements?
2. What major quality problems prevent you from meeting your customers' requirements?
3. What obstacles stand in the way of resolving these problems?
4. What would it take to resolve those problems?

Ask questions to solicit feedback about your relationship with your suppliers:

1. Who are your suppliers: Who do you depend upon for input—information, products, and/or services—to fulfill your requirements as a customer?

2. What primary inputs do you receive from the suppliers?

3. What are your requirements for those inputs?

4. How do you communicate your requirements to your suppliers?

5. How satisfied are you with your suppliers' inputs?

6. How do you provide feedback to suppliers about their performance?

Data Collection Form

Application   Step 7: Improve Process Quality

Description   The Data Collection Form is a template for collecting and recording data. It promotes consistency of data and facilitates comparisons.

Procedure

1. Establish the specific purpose of collecting this data, questions to be addressed by the data you plan to collect.

2. Identify categories of information (for example, consequences of the problem) required to address these questions.

3. Brainstorm factors that affect these categories by asking fact-finding questions about, for example, frequency, timing, location, etc.

4. Determine how data will be analyzed.

5. Multivote to reduce both lists to an appropriate and practical number. Gathering some data may help to determine appropriate categories.

6. Construct a tabular form, using categories in step two for the column headings, factors in step three for the row labels. Provide a place to record information about

   • Who collected the data

   • Where, when, and how they were collected

   • The total population if data are from a sample

Illustration

Defective Copies					
	Missing Pages	Muddy Copies	Showthrough	Pages Out of Sequence	Totals
Machine jams					
Paper weight					
Humidity					
Toner					
Condition of Originals					
Other (Specify)					
				TOTAL	

Collected by:

Date:

Place:

Formula:

Decision Matrix

Application   Step 6: Rank Improvement Opportunities and Set Objectives

Step 7: Improve Process Quality

Description   The Decision Matrix[9] is an evaluation tool, useful for assessing the relative impact of a problem or a potential solution. When used to rank problems, it helps teams to identify as action items the problem areas that affect customer and business objectives. When used to compare potential solutions, it provides insights about relative effectiveness and suggests areas where information is insufficient to make comparisons.

Procedure

1. List alternatives: problem areas or potential solutions.

2. Brainstorm selection criteria: For problems, consider customer impact, variation between customer expectations and current performance, cost of unmet expectations. For solutions, consider cost of implementation, required resources and commitments, impact on problem.

3. Rate each alternative on a scale of 1 (low) to 5 (high) for each criteria.

4. Determine overall priority by combining ratings of all criteria for each alternative.

Illustration   This illustration represents a template for a Decision Matrix to select from among a group of solutions.

Alternatives	Cost to Implement	Required Resources	Impact on Problem	Feasibility	Overall Rank
Solution A					
Solution B					
Solution C					

Flowchart

Application   Step 5: Investigate Process to Identify Improvement Opportunities

Description   A flowchart[11] is a pictorial representation of the steps in a process, useful for investigating opportunities for improvement by gaining a detailed understanding of how the process actually works. By examining how various steps in a process relate to each other, you can often uncover potential sources of troubles. Flowcharts can be applied to any aspect of the process from the flow of materials to the steps in making a sale or servicing a product.

Flowcharts are constructed with a set of conventional, easily recognized symbols. These symbols are illustrated below.

Flow Diagram Symbols

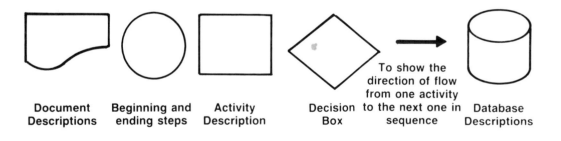

| Document Descriptions | Beginning and ending steps | Activity Description | Decision Box | To show the direction of flow from one activity to the next one in sequence | Database Descriptions |

Procedure   1. List the inputs to the process or activity.

2. For each input, ask questions such as:

  • Who supplies the input?

  • Who receives the input?

  • What is the first thing that is done with the input?

3. List the outputs from the process or activity.

4. For each output, ask questions such as:

   - Who receives this output?

   - What happens next?

5. Use the appropriate flowchart symbols to show activities and decisions involved in converting the inputs to outputs.

6. Continue building the chart until you connect into all outputs originally defined.

7. Review the chart and ask:

   - Do all work/information flows properly map into process inputs and outputs?

   - Does the chart show the serial and parallel nature of the activities?

   - Does the chart show all the potential paths work/information can take? What about special cases such as rework loops and ad-hoc procedures?

   - Does the chart accurately reflect all major decisions that are made?

   - Does the chart accurately capture what *really* happens—as distinct from how you think things should happen or how they were originally designed?

8. Date the chart for future reference and use. It should serve as a record of how the current process actually operates.

Illustration   This process flowchart illustrates the steps that might be involved in reproducing a document.

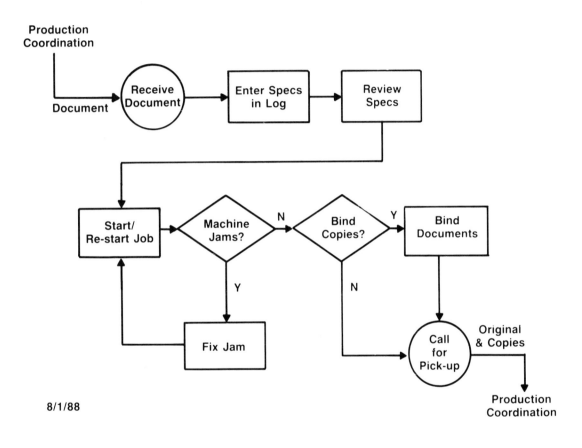

Graph

Application   Step 4: Assess Conformance to Customer Requirements

Step 6: Rank Improvement Opportunities and Set Objectives

Step 7: Improve Process Quality

Description   Graphs[9] are among the simplest and best techniques to analyze and communicate data. Graphs vary in size and form, including bar charts, line graphs, and pie charts. Common elements include:

- A title explaining what is being represented.

- A vertical or Y axis representing frequency (how many times something has happened, percentage of something, number of dollars, etc.).

- A horizontal or X axis representing the distribution or division of the data (for example, time in days, weeks, months) or another defined category (number of data points between 7.34 and 7.45), etc.

- Clear labeling for both axes.

- A scale adjusted to best illustrate the data.

- An indication of the total number of data points represented; this is indicated by $N = \rule{1cm}{0.4pt}$. As appropriate, the average of the data points should also be indicated by $\overline{X} = \rule{1cm}{0.4pt}$.

- An arrow indicating positive direction.

- Information about data collection: when, where and by whom; also, if it is a percentage or average rather than raw data points, how the data was calculated (a formula).

Bar Chart description	Bar Charts show a comparison of quantities by the relative lengths of the bars representing them. Quantities may be frequencies of events in different locations, cost of different types of breakdowns, etc.

Bar Chart procedure	1. On the horizontal axis, show the items or events being compared.
	2. On the vertical axis, show the quantities (i.e., frequency of events in different locations, cost of different types of breakdowns, etc.).

Bar Chart illustration	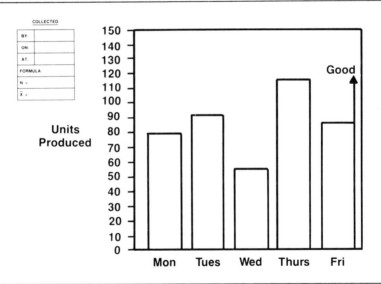

Line Graph description	Line Graphs use lines rather than bars to illustrate data. They show trend lines and display several sets of data on one chart. If several graphs are used for similar data, it is advisable to use the same scale for each.
	Line Graphs are used to monitor process performance to identify meaningful shifts in the long-range average. Line Graphs are commonly used to graph the results of a process as they vary over time.

When using a Line Graph, you should not interpret every variation in data as an important change. Rather, you should use the chart to focus on *vital long-term* changes in process performance. For instance, when a series of nine points are plotted on one side of the average, it indicates that the average has changed.

Line Graph procedure

1. Show intervals on the horizontal axis (usually time — hour, day, week, etc.).

2. Show quantities on the vertical axis (frequency of events).

3. Draw a line to connect the quantities observed on each successive interval.

If you are using several lines, use the solid black line for greatest emphasis: your own department or actual data. Dotted lines are for less emphasis, that is, other departments or projected data.

Line Graph illustration

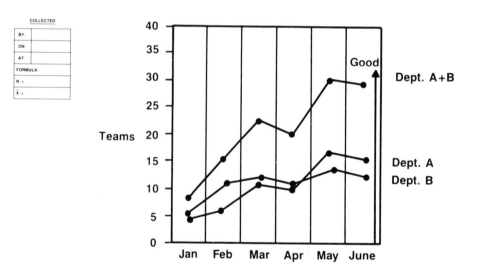

Pie Chart description

The Pie Chart shows relationships among quantities by dividing a circle into wedges (like pieces of a pie) of proportionate size. It is most useful when the whole pie (circle) represents 100 percent. The size of each wedge indicates a percentage of the whole.

Pie Chart procedure

1. Calculate the size of each wedge by dividing the value of each item by the total value of all items.

2. Multiply by 360 to determine the number of degrees for each wedge; use a protractor to plot the degrees accurately.

3. Divide a pie (circle) into wedges so that each represents the desired proportional part of the whole.

Pie Chart illustration

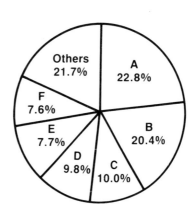

Histogram

Application Step 6: Rank Improvement Opportunities and Set Objectives

Step 7: Improve Process Quality

Description A histogram[9,14] is a visual representation of the distribution of variable data. It is useful for visually communicating information about a process and for helping to make decisions about where to focus improvement efforts.

This information is represented by a series of equal-width columns of varying heights. Because column *width* represents an interval within the *range* of observations, columns are of *equal* width. Column *height* represents the *number* of observations within a given interval. Height, therefore, *varies* proportionately from column to column. With natural data there is a tendency for many observations to fall towards the center of the distribution (central tendency), with progressively fewer as you move away from the center.

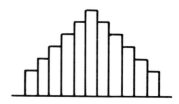

Measures of Central Tendency include:

Average — The sum of all the measured or counted data divided by the total number of data points.

Mode — the most common value or class interval grouping.

Median — the value of the data point that has an equal number of points above and below it when all the data points are arranged in ascending order of magnitude. If two values fall in the middle (even number of data points), the *median* is the *average* of the two.

Procedure

1. Collect data; count the total number of data points.

2. Arrange the data points in ascending order.

3. Determine the range of your data: subtract the smallest data point from the largest.

4. Determine the number of columns in your histogram (between 6 and 12) and divide the range (step 3) by the number of columns to determine the width of each class interval (column).

5. Put class interval scale on the horizontal axis.

6. Put frequency scale (number or percent of observations) on the vertical axis.

7. Draw the height of each column in line with the point on the vertical axis that represents the number of data points that fall within that interval. Remember that the width is the same for each column.

Illustration

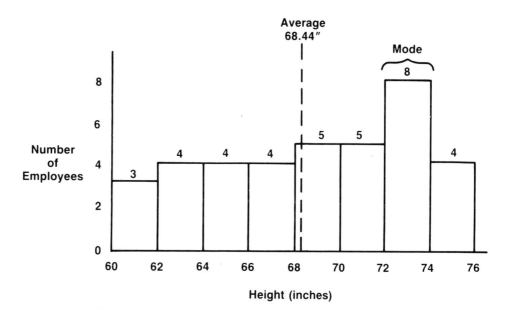

In this example:[9]

- There are 37 data points (height in inches of employees in the department). The height of the shortest employee is 60 inches, while the tallest is 75 inches. Thus the range is 15 inches:

  60, 61, 61, 62, 63, 63, 63, 64, 65, 65, 65, 66, 67, 67, 67, 68, 68, 68, 69, 69, 70, 71, 71, 71, 71, 72, 72, 72, 72, 73, 73, 73, 73, 74, 74, 74, 75

- To determine the class interval for each column on the horizontal scale, we divided 15 (the range, or the difference in inches between the tallest person and the shortest person) by 8 (the number of bars we plan to use), establishing an interval of 2. Thus, each column will include all employees within a given 2-inch range; for example, the first column will represent employees who are less than 62 inches tall, the second column, employees who are at least 62 inches but less than 64, etc.

- The highest point on our vertical scale was determined by the number of data points in the class interval with the greatest frequency or number, in this case the interval of eight employees whose height is between 72 and 74 inches.

To calculate measures of central tendency:

- Divide the sum of all data (2,532) by the number of data points (37). The **Average** = 68.44 inches.

- Count the number of people in the most populated interval (72-74). The **Mode** = 8.

- Find the value with an equal number of data points above and below, in this case 68. The **Median** = 68 inches.

Interview

Application	Step 2: Define Process and Identify Customer Requirements
	Step 3: Define and Establish Measures
	Step 4: Assess Conformance to Customer Requirements
	Step 5: Investigate Process to Identify Improvement Opportunities

Description   The interview[9] is an important information gathering technique that also fosters cooperative working relationships and encourages direct input into quality improvement efforts. Because the interviewer has an opportunity to ask follow-up questions, the interview can be one of the most effective methods for gathering more complete and useful feedback. Note that the greater the number of people you interview, the more valid your conclusions are likely to be, especially if you have a small basic population from which to select interviewees.

Procedure   1. **Before the interview:**
   - Gather background information on topic and interviewee.
   - Outline areas to be covered and major questions to be asked.
     - Open-ended questions stimulate ideas.
     - Who, what, where, when, why, and how elicit specific information.
     - "Try out" and refine questions.
   - Tell interviewee the purpose and proposed length of the interview.
   - Choose a comfortable meeting place.

2. **During the interview:**

- Help interviewee feel comfortable.

- Remain analytical and objective.

- Take notes.

- Summarize and reflect back answers to verify what you learned.

3. **After the interview:**

— Thank the interviewee.

— Review and interpret data as soon as possible (while still fresh in your mind).

Multivoting

Application	Step 1: Establish Process Management Responsibilities
	Step 3: Define and Establish Measures
	Step 4: Assess Conformance to Customer Requirements
	Step 5: Investigate Process to Identify Improvement Opportunities
	Step 6: Rank Improvement Opportunities and Set Objectives

Description Multivoting[9] is a structured series of votes used to help teams

- assign priorities in a list of many items, and
- reduce the list to a manageable few (usually three to five).

Multivoting may be used at team meetings whenever a brainstorming session has generated a list of items that is too lengthy for all to be addressed at once.

Procedure

1. Take a first vote: Each person votes for as many items as desired, but only once per item.

2. Circle the items receiving a relatively higher number of votes than the other items. (Example: A team has ten members. Items receiving five or more votes are circled).

3. Take a second vote: Each person votes for a number of items equal to one-half the total number of circled items, again only once per item. (Example: If six items received five or more votes during the first vote, then each person gets to vote three times during the second vote.)

4. Repeat steps 2 and 3 until the list is reduced to three to five items, which can be further analyzed. *Never multivote down to only one.*

Nominal Group Technique

Application   Step 1: Establish Process Management Responsibilities

Step 3: Define and Establish Measures

Step 4: Assess Conformance to Customer Requirements

Step 5: Investigate Process to Identify Improvement Opportunities

Step 6: Rank Improvement Opportunities and Set Objectives

Step 7: Improve Process Quality

Description   Nominal Group Technique[7,11] is a method of reaching consensus. It is a structured group decision-making process used to assign priorities to rank order a group of items.

Procedure   1. Silently generate ideas, in writing.

2. Record ideas without discussion.

3. Conduct group discussion *for clarification of meaning, not argument*.

4. Vote to establish the priority or rank of each item.

Two steps may be added for greater precision and consensus:

5. Discuss vote.

6. Cast final vote.

Rules for Nominal Group Technique

- Identify in advance the questions to be addressed.
- Plan to address only one topic per meeting.
- Allow no comment or discussion during the recording of ideas.
- Focus on clarification of meaning, not on arguing points, during the group discussion.
- Limit discussion, throughout the discussion phase, to brief explanations of logic or analysis of an item, and brief statements agreeing or disagreeing with the item.

Pareto Diagram

Application   Step 4: Assess Conformance to Customer Requirements

Step 5: Investigate Process to Identify Improvement Opportunities

Step 6: Rank Improvement Opportunities and Set Objectives

Step 7: Improve Process Quality

Description   A Pareto Diagram[5,11] is a simple graphical technique for rank ordering causes from most to least significant. The Pareto Diagram is based on the Pareto principle, which states that just a few of the causes often account for most of the effect. By distinguishing the critical causes—what Juran calls "the vital few"—from the potentially less significant causes, you may get maximum quality improvement with the least effort.

The Pareto Diagram displays, in decreasing order, the relative contribution of each cause to the total problem. Relative contribution may be based on the number of occurrences, the cost associated with each cause, or another measure of impact on the problem:

- Blocks are used to show the relative contribution of each cause.

- A cumulation line is used to show the cumulative contribution of causes.

Procedure   1. Select the problem to be compared or rank-ordered.

2. Select the standard unit of measurement for comparison, such as annual cost, frequency, etc.

3. Select the time period to be analyzed.

4. Gather necessary data on the occurrence of each cause (Examples: Defect A occurred ten times in the last six months, Defect B cost $100 in the last six months).

5. Compare the frequency or cost of each cause relative to all other causes (Examples: Defect A occurred 75 times, Defect B occurred 89 times, and Defect C occurred 50 times; Defect A cost $200 annually, Defect B cost $500 annually, etc.).

6. List the causes from left to right on the horizontal axis in their order of decreasing frequency or cost. You can combine the categories containing the fewest items into an "other" category. Place this category at the extreme right, as the last bar in the diagram.

7. Above each classification, draw a rectangle whose height represents the frequency or cost in that classification. If you record raw data on the left vertical axis with a percentage scale on the right vertical axis, be sure that the two axes are drawn to scale. For example, 100 percent should be opposite the total frequency or cost and 50 percent should be opposite the halfway point in the raw data.

8. To help interpret the chart, draw a line from the top of the tallest bar, moving upward from left to right. This shows the cumulative frequency of the categories.

Illustration

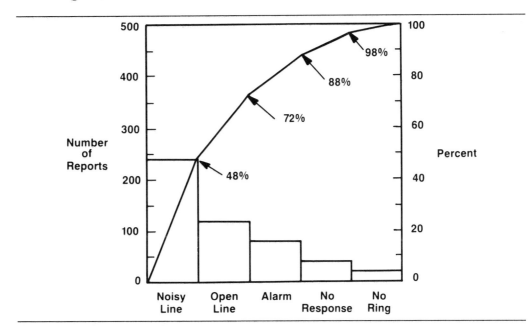

Problem Definition Checklist

Application	Step 7: Improve Process Quality

Description A well-stated problem[9] describes what is wrong in specific, concrete terms, avoiding hidden solutions. It describes the problem in terms that are

Specific: State where and when the problem is occurring. It should locate the "pain" of the problem.

Declarative: State the problem clearly and definitely, not as a question or an incomplete statement.

Quantified: State the difference between "what is" and "what should be" in measurable terms. Some problems are difficult to quantify. However, a problem that is impossible to quantify should be reexamined.

Factual Consciously avoid implicit assumptions about solution or cause; state only the facts. Any problem definition using "lack of," "due to," or similar phrasing implies a cause or solution.

The Problem Definition Checklist is helpful for developing a good problem statement.

Checklist Questions

- Does the problem definition answer the questions who, what, when, and where?
- Does the problem definition focus on the *effect*, not the *cause*, of the problem?
- Does the definition clearly describe the difference between "what is" and "what should be"?
- Does the definition describe this difference in measurable terms?
- Does the problem definition avoid broad categories?
- Is the definition positive (avoiding such phrases as "lack of")?
- Is it a declarative statement (as opposed to a question)?
- Does it focus on the "pain" aspect of the problem (how things are affected)?

Quality Map*

Application	Step 2: Define Process and Identify Customer Requirements
	Step 3: Define and Establish Measures
	Step 4: Assess Conformance to Customer Requirements

Description   Quality Map, abbreviated as Q-MAP throughout this book, is a personal computer software tool, developed by Pacesetter Software, for selecting and developing customized measures of process performance. Q-MAP's interactive database offers capabilities to help you:

- Look at your organization's function within the context of the larger organization
- Define customer/supplier relationships (including inputs to the group, outputs, key processes and work activities)
- Set up databases to gather, analyze, and report process performance data along quality, quantity, timeliness, and cost dimensions
- Identify opportunities for process improvement and productivity gains
- Assess your ongoing progress toward meeting customer satisfaction and business objectives.

For more information on Q-MAP, contact:

AT&T Internal:	AT&T Corporate	Other:	Pacesetter Software
	Education & Training		P.O. Box 5270
	Technical Education Manager		Princeton, NJ 08540
	140 Centennial Avenue		(609) 683-5225
	Piscataway, NJ 08855		
	(908) 457-7356		

---

* Quality Map is a registered trademark of Pacesetter Software, a division of Synergistic Software & Systems, Inc., Princeton, NJ.

Survey

Application   Step 2: Define Process and Identify Customer Requirements

Step 3: Define and Establish Measures

Step 4: Assess Conformance to Customer Requirements

Description   Surveys, in the context of this discussion, refer to written questionnaires. Survey participants are asked to answer questions posed by the questionnaire and to return the completed questionnaire by a specified date. Surveys, like interviews, can be an effective means of determining needs.

Although surveys historically yield a low percentage of return, you may improve response to your survey by

- personal retrieval on the due date, or
- follow-up telephone calls requesting compliance.

It is especially important, when you are surveying a small population (fewer than 25), to follow up for a high rate of response if you are to draw any meaningful conclusions from your survey response.

Procedure   1. Identify candidates to be surveyed.

2. Formulate questions and "try them out." Revise if necessary to be sure that they will elicit a useful and *unbiased* response.

3. Establish weightings for response.

4. Mail surveys.

5. Follow up to encourage response.

Tree Diagram

Application   Step 2: Define Process and Identify Customer Requirements

Description   A tree diagram[7] uses a systematic approach to define a hierarchy of needs, objectives, characteristics, or goals.

The tree diagram method is best suited to:

- Translating very ill-defined needs into operational characteristics
- Exploring all the possible causes of a problem
- Defining specific tasks to reach higher level goals.

Procedure   1. State the core issue, problem, or goal.

2. Generate all possible tasks, methods, or causes related to the statement.

3. Construct the actual tree diagram:

   - Place the central issue/goal/problem to the far left of the chart.
   - Find the ideas which are most closely related to that statement.
   - Place the ideas/tasks immediately to the right of the central issue.
   - Focus on these as central issues and repeat the task generation steps until all of the ideas are exhausted.
   - Review the tree diagram for obvious gaps in sequence or logic.
   - Review with other groups for comments and recommendations.

Illustration   This figure shows a tree diagram for producing a quality document.

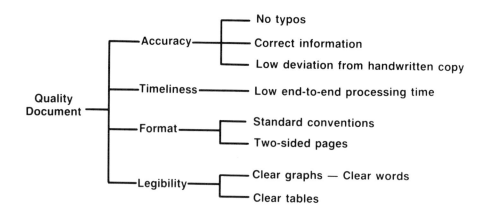

GLOSSARY

Abnormal variation Changes in process performance that cannot be accounted for by typical day-to-day variation. Also referred to as nonrandom variation.

AT&T Quality Policy Quality excellence is the foundation for the management of our business and the keystone of our goal of customer satisfaction. It is therefore our policy to:

- Consistently provide products and services that meet the quality expectations of our customers.

- Actively pursue ever-improving quality through programs that enable each employee to do his or her job right the first time.

Conformance Affirmative indication or judgement that a product or service has met specified requirements, contract, or regulation. The state of meeting the requirements.

Continuous improvement The idea that quality management and improvement is necessarily a continuous activity to ensure ongoing customer satisfaction and improved efficiency.

Control The state of stability, normal variation, and predictability. Process of regulating and guiding operations and processes using quantitative data. Control mechanisms are also used to detect and avoid potential adverse effects of change.

Corrective action The implementation of effective solutions that result in the elimination of identified product, service, and process problems.

Customer The recipient or beneficiary of the outputs of your work efforts or the purchaser of your products and services. May be either internal or external to the company.

Customer/supplier model	The model is generally represented using three interconnected triangles to depict inputs flowing into a work process that, in turn, adds value and produces outputs that are delivered to a customer. Throughout the process, requirements and feedback from the customer to the supplier monitor how well the process is meeting customer needs and expectations.
Effectiveness	The state of having produced a decided or desired effect; the state of achieving customer satisfaction.
Efficiency	A measure of performance that compares output production with cost or resource utilization (as in number of units per employee per hour or per dollar).
Expectations	Customer perceptions about how our products and services will meet specific customer needs and requirements; expectations for a product or service are shaped by many factors, including the specific use the customer intends to make of it, prior experience with a similar product or service, and our representations and commitments in, for example, marketing and advertising descriptions.
Feedback	Communication from the customer about how process output compares with customer expectations.
Functional manager	An individual responsible for coordinating the processes that comprise a business function.
Functional organization	An organization responsible for a major corporate business function, such as marketing, sales, design, manufacturing, and distribution.
Implementer	An individual working within the process who is responsible for carrying out specific job tasks.
Inputs	Products or services obtained from others (suppliers) in order to perform our job tasks.
Measurement	The act or process of measuring to compare results to requirements. A quantitative estimate of performance.

Outputs	Materials or information provided to others (internal or external customers).
Process	A set of interrelated work activities that are characterized by a set of specific inputs and value-added tasks that produce a set of specific outputs.
Process capability	Long-term performance level after the process has been brought under control.
Process Management Team (PMT)	A group of employees organized to carry out the Process Quality Management and Improvement (PQMI) methodology and to provide a focus for *continuous* quality improvement.
Process owner	Coordinates the various functions and work activities at all levels of a process, has the authority or ability to make changes in the process as required, and manages the process end-to-end so as to ensure optimal overall performance.
Process performance	A measure of how effectively and efficiently a process satisfies customer requirements.
Process review	An objective assessment of how well the PQMI methodology has been applied to your process. Emphasizes the potential for long-term process results rather than the actual results achieved.
Quality	Consistently meeting customer expectations.
Quality Consultant	An individual who has experience and expertise in applying quality tools and techniques to resolve process problems and who can advise and facilitate quality improvement teams using these tools and techniques.
Quality Council	An organization of senior managers within a business unit and management representatives of associated business functions outside the unit, who provide vision and leadership for implementing the Quality Policy within the business unit.

Quality Improvement Team (QIT)	A group of individuals charged with the task of planning and implementing process quality improvement. The three major roles in this task force are team leader, team facilitator, and team member.
Quality management	The management of a process to maximize customer satisfaction at the lowest overall cost to the company.
Quality management system	The collective plans, activities, and events that are established to ensure that a product, process, or service will satisfy given needs. The infrastructure supporting the operational process management and improvement methodology.
Quality tool	Instrument or technique that supports the activities of process quality management and improvement.
Requirements	Performance standards associated with specific and measurable customer needs; the "it" in "do it right the first time."
Root cause	Original reason for nonconformance within a process. When the root cause is removed or corrected, the nonconformance will be eliminated.
Statistical process control (SPC)	The application of statistical methods to analyze data, study, and monitor process capability and performance. Through the use of SPC methods such as control charts, you can determine if a process is in control and then keep it in control while working to achieve a new level of process performance.
Subprocesses	The internal processes that make up a process.
Suppliers	The source of the material and/or information input to a process. Suppliers can be internal or external to a company, group, or organization.

REFERENCES

[1] AT&T. 1988. *AT&T Quality Improvement Cycle.* Issue 1. (October). AT&T Quality Steering Committee.

[2] Kane, E.J. 1986. IBM's Quality Focus on the Business Process. *Quality Progress.* (April) pp. 24-33.

[3] Melan, E.H. 1985. Process Management in Service and Administrative Operations. *Quality Progress.* (June) pp. 52-59.

[4] Juran, J. M. 1986. *Juran on Quality Planning.* Wilton, Conn: Juran Institute, Inc.

[5] Juran, J.M., F. M. Gryna, and R. S. Bingham. 1974. *Quality Control Handbook.* 3d ed. New York: McGraw-Hill, Inc., pp. 2-17–2-18.

[6] Nickell, W.S. and J. S. McNeil. 1986. IBM's Process Management in a Marketing Environment. *Preprints of IMPRO86—The Juran Institute's Fourth Annual Conference on Quality Improvement.*

[7] Brassard, Michael. 1986. *Beyond the Seven Old Tools.* Seminar sponsored by Growth Opportunity Alliance of Greater Lawrence (G.O.A.L.), Lawrence, Mass.

[8] Xerox Corporation. 1987. *Competitive Benchmarking: What It Is and What It Can Do For You.* (May) Stamford, Conn: Xerox Corporate Quality Office. Reference No. 700P90201. pp. 2-10.

[9] Florida Power & Light Co. 1987. *FPL Quality Improvement Program—Team Guidebook.* (Jan). Florida Power and Light Company.

[10] Ishikawa, K. 1982. *Guide to Quality Control.* 2d ed. rev. Asian Productivity Organization.

[11] Growth Opportunity Alliance of Greater Lawrence. 1985. *The Memory Jogger.* A Pocket Guide of Tools for Continuous Improvement. Sixth Printing. Available from G.O.A.L., Lawrence, Mass. pp. 6-31.

[12] Stratton, A. Donald. 1987. Force Field Analysis: A Powerful Tool For Facilitators. *The Juran Report* No. 8. Wilton, Conn: Juran Institute, Inc.

[13] AT&T Bell Laboratories. 1987. *Quality by Design.* Issue 1.1. (July). Quality Assurance Center. p. 141.

[14] AT&T. 1986. *AT&T Statistical Quality Control Handbook.* 2d ed. 1958. Section I, part B, pp. 5-16; Section II, part F, pp. 149-156.

Supporting the Total Quality Approach:
The AT&T Quality Library

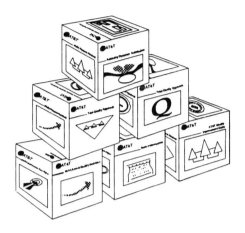

AT&T's Total Quality Approach defines the fundamental building blocks from which the business units and divisions construct their quality systems. AT&T provides resources—including the AT&T Quality Library—to help organizations adapt and augment the elements of the Total Quality Approach to meet the expectations of their customers and the needs of their business. The books of the Quality Library are available through the AT&T Customer Information Center (1-800-432-6600).

Quality Technology and Tools Series

Design for Quality and Reliability Volume(500-178)

Quality by Design (500-021)
A quality manual for the AT&T R&D community.

Reliability by Design (010-810-105)
A reliability manual for the AT&T R&D community.

Data Quality Volume (500-487)

Data Quality Foundations (500-490)
Introduction to basic concepts and dimensions of data quality.

*Describing Information Processes:
The FIP Technique* (500-488)
A complement to standard flowcharting, especially useful for understanding information processes.

*Improving Data Accuracy:
The Data Tracking Technique* (500-489)
A proven method to improve data accuracy.

Tools for Quality Management Volume (500-455)

Analyzing Business Process Data: The Looking Glass (500-445)
Help on using statistical quality control techniques to understand, control, and improve business processes.

AT&T Cost-of-Quality Guidelines (500-746)
Suggestions for estimating costs of appraisal, prevention, and corrective action and for using the data to select improvement opportunities.

AT&T Statistical Quality Control Handbook (700-444)
The classical text that has taught statistical process control to thousands worldwide.

Benchmarking Handbook (500-454)
AT&T's approach to identifying and adapting world-class practices for business and process improvement.

Quality Management and Systems Series

People, Leadership, and Involvement Volume (500-456)

AT&T's Total Quality Approach (500-452)
An overview of the quality principles and practices that underlie how AT&T manages its business to meet the needs of customers, employees, stockholders, and communities.

Batting 1000: Using Baldrige Feedback to Improve Your Business (500-451)
A strategy for using feedback from the Baldrige Award evaluation process to improve your business.

Leading the Quality Initiative (500-441)
Eight action areas that define a Quality Council's role in adapting and implementing AT&T's Total Quality Approach.

Policy Deployment Handbook (500-453)
A reference to help managers achieve break-through improvements in business capabilities by aligning improvement efforts with strategic goals to meet customer and business needs.

Quality Manager's Handbook (500-442)
A road map for the quality manager with recommended tools, references, and re-sources for building a world-class quality system.

Shared Values: Our Common Bond (500-479)
An exploration of the power of shared values, including a case study, basic concepts, and a 3-phase approach to getting started. AT&T people talk about living their values in a companion videotape, *Shared Values: Something Worth Acting For.*

Process Management and Improvement Volume (500-457)

AT&T Quality Improvement Cycle (500-031)
An eight-step approach to problem-solving and quality improvement.

Process Quality Management and Improvement Guidelines (PQMI) (500-049)
A customer-focused, seven-step cycle for management, control, and improvement of business processes.

PQMI: Tips, Experiences, and Lessons Learned (500-446)
Practical advice and examples based on AT&T experience for applying PQMI and other process management methodologies.

Quality Improvement Team Helper (500-444)
Guidelines for starting a quality improvement team.

Reengineering Handbook (500-449)
Approach to redesigning a process to make substantial improvement in meeting customer requirements and increasing efficiency.

Customer Focus Volume (500-458)

Achieving Customer Satisfaction (500-443)
A strategy for using customer and competitor information to increase customer satisfaction.

Great Performances! The Best in Customer Satisfaction and Customer Service (500-450)
A look at how world-class companies make customer satisfaction a total business strategy.

Reference Series

A History of Quality Control and Assurance at AT&T: 1920-1970
(500-721, booklet and 14 videotapes; 500-722, booklet only)
Videotaped interviews with AT&T people and their colleagues whose work advanced the development and application of quality methods.

AT&T Quality Glossary (500-745)
Definitions of terms and acronyms.

For AT&T employees only:
AT&T Quality Management Contacts Directory (500-454)
AT&T Quality Resources Directory (500-298)